PRENTICE HALL

Language Teaching Methodology Series

Classroom Techniques and Resources
General Editor: Christopher N. Candlin

Listening in Action

Other titles in this series include:

CANDLIN, Christopher and MURPHY, Dermot
Language learning tasks

ELLIS, Rod
Classroom language acquisition in context

ELLIS, Rod
Classroom second language development

FRANK, Christine and RINVOLUCRI, Mario
Grammar in action

KENNEDY, Chris
Language planning and English language teaching

KRASHEN, Stephen
Language acquisition and language education

KRASHEN, Stephen
Principles and practice in second language acquisition

KRASHEN, Stephen
Second language acquisition and second language learning

KRASHEN, Stephen and TERRELL, Tracy
The natural approach

MARTON, Waldemar
Methods in English language teaching: frameworks and options

McKAY, Sandra
Teaching grammar

NUNAN, David
Understanding language classrooms

PECK, Antony
Language teachers at work

ROBINSON, Gail
Crosscultural understanding

STEVICK, Earl
Success with foreign languages

STEMPLESKI, Susan and TOMALIN, Barry
Video in action

SWALES, John
Episodes in ESP

TAYLOR, Linda
Teaching and learning vocabulary

WALLACE, Catherine
Learning to read in a multicultural society

WENDEN, Anita and RUBIN, Joan
Learner strategies in language learning

YALDEN, Janice
The communicative syllabus

Listening in Action
Activities for developing listening in language teaching

MICHAEL ROST
Temple University

ENGLISH LANGUAGE TEACHING

Prentice Hall
New York   London   Toronto   Sydney   Tokyo   Singapore

Published 1991 by
Prentice Hall International
Campus 400, Spring Way
Maylands Avenue, Hemel Hempstead
Hertfordshire, HP2 7EZ

Typeset in Times by
MHL Typesetting Ltd, Coventry

Printed and bound in Great Britain by
Redwood Books, Trowbridge, Wiltshire

Library of Congress Cataloging-in-Publication Data

Rost, Michael.
    Listening in action / Michael Rost.
      p. cm. — (Language teaching methodology series)
    Includes indexes.
    ISBN 0-13-538778-7
    1. English language — Study and teaching — Foreign speakers.
    2. Listening. I. Title. II. Series.
    PE1128.A2R67 1991
    428'. 007—dc20   90-46348
                                                CIP

British Library Cataloguing in Publication Data

Rost, Michael
    Listening in action. — (Prentice-Hall International
language teaching methodology series).
    1. English language. Listening comprehension
    I. Title
    428.3

    ISBN 0-13-538778-7

---

9 8 7 6 5
1999 98 97 96

To Bill Landon

Contents

Preface

With the Language Teaching Methodology Series we have created a special set of books with the *In Action* title. These books are designed to offer teachers material that can be directly used in class. They are resources for action, hence the title. They offer language teachers material which can be adapted with various input for their own classroom work. The activities are presented in an accessible and teacher-friendly way, with a clear identification of teacher and learner roles and above all, they consist of tried and tested tasks. The authors of the books in the *In Action* collection all have considerable practical experience of teaching and of classroom research. It is this combination of principle and practice, available in an easily accessible form for the teacher, which characterises the design of the books. We hope that they will not only help teachers to plan and carry out exciting lessons but also to develop themselves as reflective teachers by suggesting action research that can be done with their own learners.

Listening in Action highlights the skills and strategies involved in listening in a second or foreign language. It illustrates activities which teachers can use as models to refine learners' listening ability and to develop their language learning capacity. Each activity targets a particular language level and identifies a set of specific learning goals. The activities have been organised into four major types of listening, each of which is explained in a clear and informed introduction. The activities themselves have been especially designed so that teachers are free to develop their own versions suitable for their own classes within the framework Michael Rost helpfully provides. Throughout the book the activities show how listening can be focused not only on the learning of pronunciation, vocabulary and grammatical structures but also linked to the concurrent development of other skills. Above all, the book stresses the importance of listening in context and making use of the learners' natural abilities from their mother tongue learning experience.

As General Editor, I hope that the books in this new *In Action* collection will continue the success of the Language Teaching Methodology Series more generally in developing the skills and knowledge of the reflective language teacher in the classroom.

Professor Christopher N. Candlin
General Editor

Acknowledgements

I would like to thank the many people who have helped me think through, compile and organise this book.

First, I would like to thank the series editor, Christopher Candlin, for inviting me to write a volume in this series, for providing the architecture of ideas that enabled me to plan the book, and for giving insightful feedback on the drafts which preceded the final version.

I also wish to acknowledge the assistance on this project given to me by a number of colleagues I have come to know over the past several years. Their work has enriched my ideas about teaching and about listening. In particular, I wish to thank Mary Underwood, Marc Helgesen, Penny Ur, Mario Rinvolucri, Stephen Gaies, and Jack Richards.

The work of many other colleagues has influenced my shaping of particular activities in this book. I wish to thank the following people, many of whom have been fellow participants at conferences, lectures and workshops, in teacher training seminars and in graduate courses:

Francis Bailey

Malcolm Benson

Steve Brown

Judith Coppock Gex

Paul Davis

Leslie Dickinson

Pat Dunkel

Dale Griffee

Ken Kanatani

Ellen Kisslinger

Nobuhiro Kumai

John Lance

Tim Lane

Michael Legutke

Fred Ligon

J.D. Lippett

Jack Lonergan

Alan Maley

Christine Nelson

Donna E. Norton

Ted Plaister

Susan Stempleski

Ken Stratton

Barry Tomalin

Mune Uruno

Roger von Oech

Jim Weaver

Finally, I would like to thank Jack Yohay for his valuable editorial help and Keiko Kimura for her technical assistance. I also wish to thank the staff of Prentice Hall International, and especially David Haines, Isobel Fletcher de Téllez and Angela Bryce, for their professional guidance and friendly support in planning and producing this book.

M.R.

INTRODUCTION

Introduction

Listening in Action is about 'action' in three senses:

First, *Listening in Action* stresses that *listening is an active process*. To become better listeners, our learners must employ *active thinking* as they listen. By developing an 'active attitude' about understanding and 'active strategies' for making sense of what they hear, our learners can and will improve. We, as teachers, can help our learners to develop this orientation through principled planning of activities and through attentively responding to their efforts.

Second, *Listening in Action* emphasises that *listening plays an active part in language learning*. Listening is involved in many language-learning activities, both inside and outside the language classroom. Progress in listening will provide a basis for development of other language skills. By becoming aware of the links between listening and other skills and by consistently pointing out these links to our learners, we can assist our learners in their overall language development.

Third, *Listening in Action* features *the teacher as an active 'researcher' of listening development*. As teachers, we should be active not just in planning and preparing activities for our learners, but in giving useful feedback to them and exploring with them how their listening skills are changing and improving.

Listening in Action, then, is for language teachers with the following goals:

- To help their learners become more active in developing listening skills.
- To help their learners utilise opportunities both inside and outside the classroom for becoming better listeners and better language learners.
- To improve their teaching by exploring with their students the process of learning to listen.

What is listening?

In order to define listening, we can ask two basic questions: *What are the component skills in listening?* and *What does a listener do?*

In terms of the necessary *components*, we can list the following:

- discriminating between sounds
- recognising words
- identifying grammatical groupings of words
- identifying 'pragmatic units' — expressions and sets of utterances which function as whole units to create meaning
- connecting linguistic cues to paralinguistic cues (intonation and stress) and to non-

linguistic cues (gestures and relevant objects in the situation) in order to construct
meaning
- using background knowledge (what we already know about the content and the
form) and context (what has already been said) to predict and then to confirm
meaning
- recalling important words and ideas

Successful listening involves an *integration of these component skills*. In this sense,
listening is a coordination of the component skills, not the individual skills themselves.
This integration of these perception skills, analysis skills, and synthesis skills is what
we will call a person's *listening ability*.

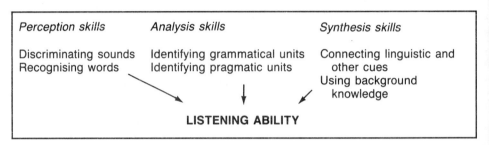

Even though a person may have good listening ability, he or she may not always
be able to understand what is being said. In order to understand messages, some
conscious action is necessary to use this ability effectively in each listening situation.
This action that a listener must perform is 'cognitive' or mental, so it is not possible
to view it directly, but we can see the effects of this action. The underlying action
for successful listening is *decision making*. The listener must make these kinds of
decisions:

- What kind of situation is this?
- What is my plan for listening?
- What are the important words and units of meaning?
- Does the message make sense?

Successful listening requires making effective 'real time' decisions about these
questions. In this sense, listening is primarily a thinking process — *thinking about
meaning*. Effective listeners develop a useful way of thinking about meaning as they
listen. The way in which the listener makes these decisions is what we will call a
listening strategy.

In order to develop a comprehensive image of ourselves as instructors of listening,
we need a combined approach for building up essential skills and for fostering successful
strategies.

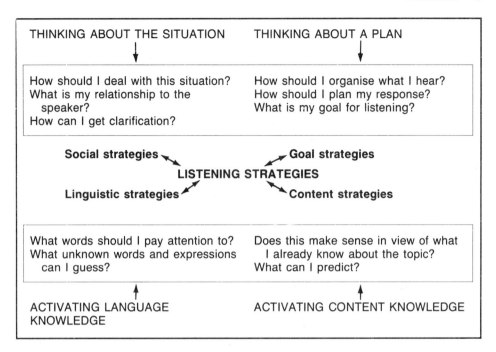

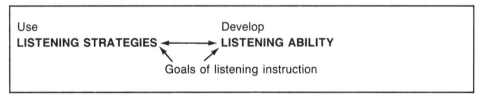

Learning styles

To develop their listening ability, our learners need a great deal of exposure to spoken language and ample practice in various listening situations. However, in addition to exposure and practice, it is vitally important for the listener to *become engaged in the process of listening* and develop a *desire to understand*. This is not something that exposure and practice alone can bring about. The ways in which individual learners try to become engaged and try to understand and try to improve are called *learning styles*.

Let us look at some different types of learners and how they approach the development of their own listening ability:

Ulla: I like to watch American films on video tape. I replay important scenes again and again until I feel that I have understood well. Then, after watching the whole film, I go back to some of the scenes — my favourite ones — and listen to them and study the language carefully. I make sure that I know exactly what the speakers say. This helps me to understand the expressions when I hear them again.

Agbo: I like to talk with people. Whenever I have free time, I try to meet English-speaking friends. Even though I'm not a good speaker or listener, I try to understand and ask a lot of questions if I want to understand something more clearly. Especially, I have one or two good friends, and by talking with them, I think my listening is getting much better. I'm certainly becoming more confident when I am with them and more comfortable with my English ability.

Emi: My listening has improved because, in my English class, we have to do a lot of talking to our classmates in English, and we have to listen to different kinds of tapes and get the important ideas. I need this kind of guidance because I would probably give up if I studied by myself. I like to be tested by the teacher about the precise meaning of the speakers on the tape, and then hear the tape again. Each time, I feel I am understanding more and becoming a better English listener.

Truyen: Although I studied English for many years, I never really understood spoken English very well. But when I entered the university, I really began to make progress with my listening ability. I think this is mainly because I am very interested in my classes. The ideas of the lectures are very difficult, but I have found that if I really want to understand the lectures, I must prepare very hard for them in advance. Sometimes I tape-record lectures and review the parts where I was confused. The preparation and the review helps me to listen better each time.

We can see some clear differences in these types of learners. Ulla might be called a 'self-instruction type'. She sees useful opportunities for learning alone, she consistently carries out her plans, and she enjoys the learning process. She has developed her ability to perceive language accurately and has worked on developing her memory for English vocabulary. She also knows how to assess her own progress.

Agbo is what might be called a 'social type'. He enjoys face-to-face interaction and senses that it is an effective way to get 'the real thing' in terms of listening practice. He is usually satisfied to get the general gist of what he hears, though he is not embarrassed to ask questions if he wants to understand specific expressions and meanings. He understands that language development requires consistent effort and he is willing to make that effort.

Emi is what might be called a 'language classroom type'. She trusts her teachers to present her with useful practice. She consistently tries hard to do what is expected of her. She has a sense of what her goals are and feels strongly that classroom instruction is helping her to reach them. She is confident that she will succeed.

Truyen is what we might call a 'subject matter type'. He wants to listen better so that he has access to ideas in English. He is, in this sense, 'listening to learn', not just 'learning to listen'. He sees English not just as a vehicle of social communication, but as a carrier of important concepts, and an aid to him in his career. He has found a motivation and a systematic method for developing his listening ability.

Principles for developing listening ability

We can identify different strengths in the learning styles of each of these four types of learners. All of these styles contain useful learning strategies and illustrate important learning principles. From these portraits, and based on what we know about language skill development, we can draw up some general guidelines:

1. *Listening ability develops through face-to-face interaction.*
   By *interacting* in English, learners have the chance for new language input and the chance to check their own listening ability. Face-to-face interaction provides stimulation for development of listening for meaning.

2. *Listening develops through focusing on meaning and trying to learn new and important content in the target language.*
   By focusing on meaning and *real reasons for listening* in English, learners can mobilise both their linguistic and non-linguistic abilities to understand.

3. *Listening ability develops through work on comprehension activities.*
   By focusing on *specific goals* for listening, learners can evaluate their efforts and abilities. By having well-defined comprehension activities, learners have opportunities for assessing what they have achieved and for revision.

4. *Listening develops through attention to accuracy and an analysis of form.*
   By learning to perceive sounds and words *accurately* as they work on meaning-oriented activities, our learners can make steady progress. By learning to hear sounds and words more accurately, learners gain confidence in listening for meaning.

What can a language teacher do to help students develop their listening ability?

As teachers, we need a comprehensive image of what we do in order to help students develop their listening ability. Recalling the earlier discussion about listening development, we can propose several guidelines for the classroom teacher in assisting students to develop their listening.

General

1. Talk to your students in English. Talk to *all* of your students — not just the better

English speakers. Make English a vital language for communication. Personalise the classroom: get to know your students through talking with them about topics of mutual interest.

2. Make English the language of your classrom. Give opportunities in class for the students to *exchange ideas* with each other in English. Point out to them how they are becoming confident and effective *users* of English.

3. Introduce your class to other speakers of English — personally or through use of video and audio tapes. Expose them to different types of people and situations. Above all, encourage them to listen to understand things that are important to them.

4. Encourage the learners to become independent, to seek out listening opportunities on their own *outside of the classroom*. Help them to identify ways of using English language media (TV and radio broadcasts, video tapes). Set up a self-access listening and learning centre. Help your students to develop self-study listening programmes and goals.

In the classroom

1. Set activities for listening that personally *engage your students*. Set challenging, yet realistic, goals for each activity. Give the students clear feedback on how well they do. Provide systematic review of tapes and activities to help consolidate their learning and memory.

2. Focus on teaching, rather than on testing. Reward students for trying to come up with reasonable ideas, rather than just 'the correct answer' during listening activities. Keep a record of what the students have *achieved* during the course.

3. Look for effective ways to *utilise audio and video tapes* that come with textbooks you are using. With some thought and experimentation with different types of listening exercises, you will find relevant and productive uses for these tapes. (The index in this book will direct you to ideas for utilising audio and video tapes.)

Teaching procedures

For classroom teaching, it is important to have a model of instruction that incorporates useful learning principles. Most experienced teachers seem to have a model of the 'ideal' sequence they will follow in a class — although in practice they will usually skip back and forth between steps in response to what their students do. A general model for a sequence in a listening phase of a class is given on the next page.

Listening in Action will provide you with a menu of many specific ideas and formulas for setting up complete listening activities with your students. Of course, you, the teacher, must select wisely from the menu and adapt these ideas in light of

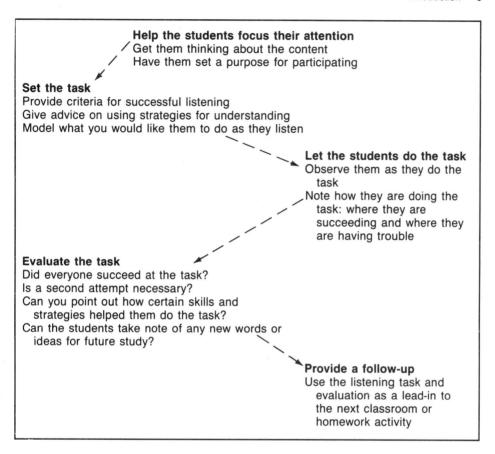

Help the students focus their attention
Get them thinking about the content
Have them set a purpose for participating

Set the task
Provide criteria for successful listening
Give advice on using strategies for understanding
Model what you would like them to do as they listen

Let the students do the task
Observe them as they do the task
Note how they are doing the task: where they are succeeding and where they are having trouble

Evaluate the task
Did everyone succeed at the task?
Is a second attempt necessary?
Can you point out how certain skills and strategies helped them do the task?
Can the students take note of any new words or ideas for future study?

Provide a follow-up
Use the listening task and evaluation as a lead-in to the next classroom or homework activity

what you know of *your students* and *your own teaching situation* and *teaching goals*. Experiment with the activities and evaluate them in light of your own teaching experience. Adjust subsequent activities in order to find the right level of challenge for your students. In this way, *Listening in Action* will work best for you and for your students.

Organisation of *Listening in Action*

Listening in Action is divided into four main sections:

Section I.   *Attentive listening*

Section II.   *Intensive listening*

Section III.   *Selective listening*

Section IV.   *Interactive listening*

Each section helps students develop a range of skills and strategies.

Section I: *Attentive listening* is designed to give students practice with listening and with supplying short responses to the speaker, either verbally or non-verbally (through actions). Because this kind of 'responsive' listening involves immediate processing of information and quick decisions about how to respond, the activities in Section I provide a great deal of support to help the learners 'process' the information they hear. The support is of three types: *linguistic*, in the form of cue words and previewed utterances, *non-linguistic*, in the form of visual aids, photographs, tangible objects and music used in the activity, and *interactional*, in the form of repetitions, paraphrases and confirmation checks by the speaker. By providing this support, the activities allow the teacher to introduce real-time listening practice to students at all levels, including beginners. Because the support in each activity can be varied, teachers can utilise these activities with more proficient students as well, to help them increase their attention span for spoken English.

Section II: *Intensive listening* will focus the students' attention on language form. The aim of this section is to raise the learners' awareness of how differences in sound, structure, and lexical choice can affect meaning. Because this kind of listening involves an appreciation of how form affects meaning, all of the activities in this section are contextualised — placed in a real or easily imagined situation. In this way, all students — even beginners — can practise intensive listening in a context of language use, from which it is most likely to transfer to 'real life' listening situations. Because the activities in this section require attention to specific *contrasts* of form — grammatical, lexical, or phonological — the teacher can easily adapt the activities to more proficient students by increasing the complexity of the language forms.

Section III: *Selective listening* will help enable students to identify a purpose for listening. By providing focused information-based tasks, the activities in Section III help direct the students' attention on key words, discourse sequence cues, or 'information structures' (exchanges in which factual information is given). By learning to attend to words, cues, and facts *selectively*, students at all levels come to handle short naturalistic texts (such as announcements) as well as longer and more complex texts (such as authentic video programmes). Because the task support in these activities can be adjusted, Section III is useful for students at all proficiency levels.

Section IV: *Interactive listening* is designed to help learners assume active roles in shaping and controlling an interaction, even when they are in the 'listener's role'. Because it is important for learners to take an active role as listeners, each activity in this section has a built-in need for information or clarification questions by the listener. In order to work toward the goal of active participation by the listener, the students themselves — rather than the teacher or an audio or video tape — become the focus of the activities. To this end, in Section IV, listening skills are developed in the context of interaction — mainly through information gap pair work, jigsaw groups, and student presentations and reports.

The introductions to each of the four sections (see pages 21, 49, 81, and 121) provide fuller explanations of the purposes of each section and the rationale for the specific activities.

Sequencing the four sections

The four sections (Attentive Listening, Intensive Listening, Selective Listening, and Interactive Listening) *may* be used in this given sequence, in order to provide a 'natural' progression from activities that entail minimal verbal interaction to those that involve a maximum of interaction. However, since learners' background in language study, current learning needs and classroom expectations will vary, it is recommended that the four sections be used *interactively*, with appropriate activities drawn from each section according to the learning requirements and readiness of the students.

One goal of any classroom activity is to provide the *optimal challenge* for the students. Since learners' listening abilities will vary, teachers should note how the activities can be adapted to the learners' capabilities. The main techniques of adjusting the 'level' of an activity are the following:

1. Make the 'input' language of the activity simpler or less complex.

   This can be done most effectively by slowing down your speech (using longer pauses between groups of words) in order to allow the learners more salient boundaries between grammatical constituents and to give them more time to process the language; by repeating familiar information; by clearly signalling (through intonation and use of discourse markers) shifts in the text; by paraphrasing unfamiliar vocabulary.

2. Create pre-listening activities that give a useful preview of the content and procedures in the activity.

   This can be done by providing some of the difficult language items (grammar structures and vocabulary) in advance; by stating clearly the students' purpose for listening; by providing some advance question—answer or dictation activities that use the key vocabulary items; by having a warm-up chat with the students which relates to the topic.

3. Give visual support for the listening activity.

   This could be accomplished through the use of maps, graphs, illustrations, photographs, film strips, or (silent) video. The instructor's gestures, facial expressions and other body language can lend visual support to a listening activity as well.

4. Break down the steps of the activity in order to provide sub-goals.

   This can be achieved by having the students listen several times, each time with *just one goal* to accomplish (e.g. identifying the number of speakers, identifying the main topic words, identifying whether a particular expression occurs in the text).

5. Decrease the amount of oral or written production that is required of the students during the listening phase of the activity.

   This can be accomplished by requiring only non-verbal responses (e.g. 'raise your hands when you hear . . .') or by using visual icons that the students select to represent their response (e.g. ticking a smiling face on a worksheet means 'True' or 'I agree with the speaker').

Using *Listening in Action*

Each section has a separate introduction, with the following features:

1. It gives an **overview** of the activity goals and explains the rationale for the organisation of the section.

2. It highlights the **key features** of the activities and shows how these features relate to the goals of the section.

3. It **previews the activities** in the section and indicates the links between activities.

   Following the introduction, each section contains several individual activity outlines.

1. They provide an introductory heading to suggest appropriateness of the activity for:

   • level (elementary, intermediate, or advanced) — a *relative* level of proficiency to indicate for whom the main activity is most suitable;
   • student age (children — ages 8–12; young adults — ages 13–17; adults — over 18) — the group(s) for whom the main activity is most suitable;
   • purpose of the activity (in terms of listening skills or strategies to be practised);
   • text type (the source of the 'input' for the activity).

2. They offer an overview of the classroom action — what the students actually will do (see: **In this activity** . . .).

3. They detail steps in the teacher's preparation of the activity (see: **Preparation**).

4. They set out the main steps for carrying out the activity in class (see: **In class**).

5. They outline variations offering similar types of practice (Note: often these are variations of the main activity that will be suitable for different age groups or proficiency levels) (see: **Variations**).

6. They offer useful follow-up options to consolidate learning (see: **Follow-up options**).

7. They propose possible links to other activities in the book (see: **Links**).

8. They suggest some general evaluation questions for the teacher (see: **Teacher's diary**).

In order to use *Listening in Action* effectively, it is recommended that you read through the introduction to each section for a general orientation first. After you have read the section introduction and have considered the main features of the type of listening practice featured, consider which activities from that section will be most suitable for your students.

Once you familiarise yourself with the four main sections of the book, you may wish to locate suitable activities by using the indexes at the back of the book. They provide an initial summary of each activity in the book (Index A), as well as various options for access to the activities:

*   Type of activity (such as following instructions, taking notes, or filling in information charts) (Index B)
*   Sources for the activities (such as news broadcasts or lectures) (Index C)
*   Language level of the student group (beginning, intermediate, advanced) (Index D)
*   Student age (children, young adults, adults) (Index E)
*   Medium of the input (audio tape, video tape, or 'live') (Index F)

One additional feature of *Listening in Action* that can be of great use to you as a teacher is the *Teacher's diary* and *Links* section at the end of each activity outline. In this part of the activity, you are asked to reflect briefly on evaluation questions such as the following:

*   How did the activity go?
*   How did your students do?
*   What difficulties did they have?
*   What aspects of the activity were most useful?
*   What aspects of the activity would you choose to revise?

The questions provided serve as a framework for reflection and evaluation of the activity, not as literal questions that must be answered explicitly. However, by taking time to write out responses to some of the questions in a separate notebook (or directly in the book), you will be clarifying your own thoughts and providing concrete teaching notes for your future classes.

In addition, by taking time to evaluate your classroom activities in this way and by considering different possible linking activities in the *Links* section, you will be participating in a kind of 'action research' that both you and your students will find rewarding — as part of your teaching and as part of your students' learning.

For further reading

Many teachers will want to explore listening further and find links to language learning research beyond their own classrooms, to teaching methodologies, and to materials development. Below are brief descriptions of several books (in alphabetical order by author) which address various aspects of listening. You may wish to select one or more books on this list for further reading. The list here is by no means exhaustive; it is, rather, intended to be an introductory sample. By 'following the trail' of references that these authors provide (including references to key articles in language teaching and applied linguistics journals), you will be able to explore further many of the issues raised in *Listening in Action*.

Ann Anderson and Tony Lynch, *Listening*, Oxford University Press, 1988.

This book features an interactive format for developing observation and classroom research skills in the reader. The authors lead you (the reader) through a series of short, informative essays and interactive tasks which allow you to explore, in a very practical way, such questions as: *What is successful listening? What listening skills do native speakers use? What comprehension problems do second language learners experience?* The authors provide a helpful scheme for grading listening exercises and review several examples of classroom listening materials.

Gillian Brown, *Listening to Spoken English (second edition)*, Longman, 1990.

This volume, written by one of the leading researchers on listening in educational settings, provides a thorough analysis of the language problems second language listeners need to overcome in order to learn to understand spoken English. The author describes the functions of rhythm and intonation and sets forth very clearly the common patterns of sound simplifications that occur in connected speech. The volume also provides recommendations for a programme to teach comprehension of spoken English.

Gillian Brown and George Yule, *Teaching the Spoken Language*, Cambridge University Press, 1983.

This book provides an important link between research into listening processes and classroom teaching. Based on research the authors conducted (with first and second language speakers of English), the book separates spoken language into 'interactional' and 'transactional' components and shows how the educational and cultural background of the listener, the context or setting of the discourse, and the 'co-text' (other language elements which are in the discourse) are involved in listening comprehension. One chapter is devoted exclusively to classroom teaching of listening comprehension and features an approach to grading materials for 'transactional' (information-based) discourse.

J. Marvin Brown and Adrian S. Palmer, *The Listening Approach*, Longman, 1988.

This book presents an experimental application of the 'natural approach' to language teaching, an approach which emphasises giving massive amounts of 'comprehensible input' to students before speaking is expected to emerge. The authors report on their work in an experimental curriculum in Thailand and provide outlines of the classroom procedures, projects, demonstrations and stories that were developed.

Joan Morley, *Listening and Language Learning in ESL: Developing self-study activities for listening comprehension*, Center for Applied Linguistics, Prentice Hall, 1984.

This book, written by one of the American pioneers of listening as a curriculum component, provides an interesting historical overview of the teaching of listening, with special reference to listening approaches in American ESL settings. The author sets forth a series of guiding principles for teachers of listening and gives detailed examples of 'notional—informational' listening practices that can be used in the classroom or for self-study.

David Nunan, *Designing Communicative Tasks for the Language Classroom*, Cambridge University Press, 1988.

This book offers a treatment of listening as a communicative skill. The author, widely recognised as an expert in curriculum development, analyses listening as an interactive skill and suggests an outline for measuring listening proficiency. The main part of the book presents and develops an approach to designing classroom tasks. The author demonstrates how all macro-skills (including listening) can be integrated into a communicative syllabus.

Anthony Peck, *Language Teachers at Work*, Prentice Hall, 1988.

This book compares the teaching routines of different language teachers and includes a discussion of how they handle listening exercises differently — and why they do so. Among the variables for listening exercises which are identified are 'manner of presentation' (use of tape recorder or live presentation by the teacher), use of expectation-setting exercises, directing the listening through tasks or questions, and means of checking comprehension.

Jack C. Richards, *The Language Teaching Matrix*, Cambridge University Press, 1990.

This book provides a 'multi-dimensional view' of language teaching as an interaction of curriculum, methodology, and teaching materials. One chapter looks specifically at the design of instructional materials for teaching listening comprehension. A framework for development of materials is provided, based on the psychological distinction between top—down and bottom—up processing.

Michael Rost, *Listening in Language Learning*, Longman, 1990.

This book outlines the personal, social, and educational issues that underlie the development of listening ability. After reviewing psychological aspects of listening (sound perception, decoding, and inference) and social aspects of listening (listener roles and types of listener response), the book provides a discussion of the place of listening in the language curriculum, the design of listening tasks, and testing listening ability.

Susan Sheerin, *Self-Access*, Oxford University Press, 1989.

This practical book, one in a series of resource books for teachers, provides helpful outlines for setting up a self-study centre in which students can practise various skills, including listening skills. Ideas for listening (under the heading 'Receptive Skills') include: *Self-assessment, How to use a tapescript, How to use comprehension questions*, and *What kind of learner are you?*

Earl Stevick, *Success with Foreign Languages*, Prentice Hall, 1989.

This book represents varied case studies of successful language learners. In each learner profile it is possible to see the relative importance of the role of listening development in the learner's overall language development and to learn firsthand — from the learners themselves — viable long-term approaches to listening development. Readers will be encouraged to set up their own case studies of individual language learners.

Mary Underwood, *Teaching Listening*, Longman, 1989.

This volume features a discussion of the importance of listening in language development and the importance of the teacher's role in teaching listening. The author, well-known as a teacher trainer and as a materials writer, presents an analysis of classroom teaching of listening as consisting of three stages: pre-listening, while-listening, and post-listening. Examples from published materials are given in order to illustrate principles for planning each of these stages.

Penny Ur, *Teaching Listening Comprehension*, Cambridge University Press, 1984.

This book, one of the earliest teacher handbooks to outline the classroom teaching of listening in a comprehensive way, features an analysis of the key features of 'real-life' listening and proposes that classroom instructors should aim to incorporate these features into listening exercises. Numerous examples of exercise types are given under the headings of 'Listening for perception' (at the word level and at the sentence level) and 'Listening for comprehension' (listening and making no response, listening and making short responses, and listening and making longer responses).

Jane Willis, *Teaching English through English*, Longman, 1981.

Many teachers who are non-native speakers of English are hesitant to use English in their classrooms, thus depriving students of an important opportunity for listening development. This book examines the important role of classroom English in formal language learning and shows teachers how to develop their social, personal, and organisational uses of English in the classroom. This book provides convenient reference tables of classroom language for various functions.

SECTION I

ATTENTIVE LISTENING

Introduction

Listening is an active process requiring participation on the part of the listener. Poor understanding results when listeners do not pay attention. Listeners may experience a lapse of attention for a variety of reasons: they may lose interest in the topic or the activity, they cannot keep up with what is going on, they have lost track of their goals for listening, or they are thinking too much about their own response instead of concentrating on what is being said.

Attentiveness is a necessary *condition* for understanding. Therefore you, as the teacher, must find listening activities that keep the students interested and attentive and that provide *appropriate challenge*. The activities in this section aim to help you develop your students' attentiveness in three ways:

1. By *personalising* the content of the listening activities — activities which are directed at the learners as persons and as active participants have a greater likelihood of maintaining the students' interest and motivation.

2. By keeping up a *flow of the target language*; by having the teacher use English (the target language) during activities, exclusively if possible.

3. By *lessening the stress* many students may experience in listening activities if they feel they will be called upon to repeat or give detailed oral or written responses.

In this light, the **key features** of the activities in this section are:

- Teacher and students have *face-to-face interaction*.
- The teacher uses immediate, visual, *tangible topics*.
- The teacher provides *clear procedures* for the learners.
- The teacher requires *minimal use of written language* during the activity.

- The learners listen in '*short chunks*'.
- The learners give *immediate and ongoing responses*.
- The *learners control the pace* of the activity through their responses.

There are eight basic activity outlines in this section. Most of the activities have variations which are alternative activities with similar instructional goals.

1. **Classroom language**
   Variation 1.1: Classroom management

2. **Demonstrations**
   Variation 2.1: Leader says

21

3. **Music images**
   Variation 3.1: Similar tunes

4. **Personal stories**
   Variation 4.1: Just narration
   Variation 4.2: Video documentary

5. **Questions, please!**
   Variation 5.1: Question pauses
   Variation 5.2: Interruptions
   Variation 5.3: Story boards

6. **Who's who?**
   Variation 6.1: Blip!
   Variation 6.2: Event squares

7. **Listening skits**
   Variation 7.1: Scenes

8. **Interview**
   Variation 8.1: Famous person

While all of the activities are designed for classroom use, they all have direct *links to activities outside the classroom* as well. Learners will recognise the links between these activities and 'real-world' activities such as:

- giving and receiving instructions
- watching documentary programmes
- interviewing and being interviewed
- participating in social activities

By coming to participate successfully in the attentive listening exercises in this section, learners will be preparing for participation in these real-world activities as well.

All of the activities in this section are designed for use with students of all levels, from beginning level up to advanced. Activities such as *Demonstrations*, *Who's who?* and *Interview* will be particularly useful for beginning students. However, students at intermediate and advanced levels will benefit more from these same listening activities provided that they are **appropriately graded**. In general, all of the attentive listening activities can be *graded for more advanced students* by these means:

- Increasing the pace of the activity.
- Increasing the amount and complexity of the language 'input'.
- Following up the activities with opportunities for student production.

For example, attentive listening activities such as *Questions, please* and *Listening skits*, both based on stories, are readily adaptable to intermediate and advanced levels by (1) providing a time limit for the activity, (2) making the 'input stories' more complex, and (3) using follow-up activities in which the students compose their own stories and skits.

Your students should find the activities in this section 'easy' in that they make few demands on language production (speaking and writing). Especially for learners who have had little exposure to spoken English for communicative purposes, these attentive listening activities may provide them with the necessary first step for communicative language development.

1 Classroom language

Level	Elementary and above, depending on input
Students	All ages
Purpose	Provide phrases for use during all classroom exercises
Text type	Teacher's prepared instructions

In this activity ...

The students learn clarification questions that can be used in the classroom during any speaking or listening activity.

Preparation

1. Find several large sheets of paper to post on the walls of the classroom.

2. At the top of each sheet, write these headings (or appropriate paraphrases):

    - *If you don't understand someone ...*
    - *If you want to interrupt someone ...*

    - *When you are working together in groups ...*
    - *When you need something ...*

    - *When you want to tell the teacher something ...*
    - *When you want to ask the teacher something ...*

3. Under each heading, write two or three useful phrases. Think of phrases that you would like the learners to be able to use for each function or in each setting. The list need not be exhaustive, merely a starter. You can add to it in class, as different needs for expressions come up. Possible starters are:

    > *If you don't understand ...*

    > *Excuse me, (Mr Bradley,) I have a question about this.*
    > *I'm sorry. I didn't catch the part about (...)*
    > *Did you say (...) or (...)?*
    > *Sorry to interrupt, but ...*

In class

1. At the beginning of class, post the sheets on the walls. Tell the students that these are some English expressions they can use in the class. Ask them if they know others.

2. Stand by each sheet, and pronounce the sentences. Be sure the students have the general idea of what each means. Some students may want to repeat the phrases, to be more sure of how to say them.

3. Quiz the students: *What would you say if . . . (you didn't understand something)?*

4. During classroom activities, encourage the students to look to the charts if they need help saying something in English. (You may also wish to have the students copy the charts in their own notebooks.)

> NOTE: *Because using English as the classroom language may be new for many students, even the more advanced students may not be familiar with precise and appropriate ways to address the teacher, ask questions, manage conversations in group activities, and carry out other basic communicative functions. This type of introduction of phrases, while time-consuming at first, is worthwhile in the long run.*

Variation 1.1: Classroom management

Post a list of the sentences that you will often use in the classroom for taking attendance, enquiring about absences, setting up activities, giving homework assignments, correcting errors, and giving advice. This overview of classroom functions may help the students catch on more quickly to English as the classroom language. Again, you will want to add to the list as new expressions come up during the course.

Links

Consider trying activities 2, 4 and 6 as a follow-up to this activity.

Teacher's diary

How important is the students' understanding of English for classroom management? Do your students seem to understand your directives and casual comments in English? Which of the expressions you posted seem most essential?

2 Demonstrations

Level	Elementary and above, depending on input
Students	All ages
Purpose	Develop ability to respond quickly to directives; listen for gist
Text type	Teacher's prepared instructions; recipes, directions

In this activity ...

The students watch a demonstration of an action sequence. They demonstrate their understanding through participation, performing non-verbal actions or giving short verbal responses.

Preparation

1. Think of several activities that can be demonstrated to the class. Examples are daily activities such as preparing certain foods (*making sandwiches, cooking omelettes, making instant noodles*), special activities such as operating, repairing, or assembling a machine (*taking apart a desk lamp to replace a wire, putting film in a camera, operating a remote-controlled toy car*), and unusual activities requiring special abilities such as *performing card tricks*. Select several activities that can realistically be demonstrated in class, preferably with actual props. Groups of related activities are preferable — for example, three or four cooking activities or three or four assembling activities.

2. List all the steps that are required for each activity that you will demonstrate. For example, to make a cheese sandwich: (1) Take a loaf of bread from the shelf and put it on the counter. (2) Take a bread knife from the drawer. (3) Slice two pieces of bread. Read the list aloud to yourself as you go through the sequence of actions. Have you left anything out? Prepare a sheet with the heading of each activity you will demonstrate in class. Number the sheet under each heading. Each number will represent one key step in the activity.

In class

1. Using actual props or visual aids (if props are unavailable), prepare to demonstrate the first activity. Start by introducing the activity (for example, *I'm going to show you how to make a cheese sandwich*). Indicate the necessary items and tell the students what they are called. (*You'll need a loaf of bread, cheese, a knife, and a plate.*) Tell the students how many steps you will expect them to recall — and mime — later.

2. As you say each step in the activity, ask the students to perform the activity or mime it. Encourage the students to do the activity as you say it, not in advance. (In a large class, it may be more effective to have a small participant group and a large observer group, with alternating members in the participant group.)

3. After you have directed the students through three or four action sequences, distribute the sheet with headings of the activities and the number of steps. Go back through each activity. Call out the number of the step and see if the students can recall it and mime it. Say the step again as the students are miming it. For beginning students, ask them to write down only the key verb for each step with a simple illustration. Intermediate students may be able to write out the full step.

Variation 2.1: Leader says

A popular children's game that involves following commands is 'Simon says'. In this game, the children are to follow the directions only if the teacher prefaces the command with 'Simon says'. (For example, 'Simon says to touch your toes.') As with all children's language games, it is best to first get the children involved and actually doing the activity, and *then* to work on having them understand and follow the rules!

Follow-up options

1. Ask questions about each demonstration. For beginning students, the questions might require only short answers: *Do you ever eat sandwiches for lunch? Do you make them yourself? What do you like to put in them? Do you make them in the same way as we did today?*

2. Let some students demonstrate the activity to the class, narrating as they do it. Provide assistance, or have other students provide assistance, as necessary.

3. Ask the students to prepare their own demonstrations of activities for the next class. Choose a theme such as 'recipes', 'machines', or 'daily activities'. By using the same theme, similar vocabulary items will be repeated.

Links

Consider trying activities 5, 12 and 26 as a follow-up to this activity.

Teacher's diary

Which demonstrations worked best? Where did the students have trouble? Were your directions too general? Too specific? How would you revise the activity knowing what you do now?

3　Music images

Level　　　　Intermediate and advanced

Students　　Young adults

Purpose　　Develop visualisation and imagination while listening

Text type　Audio tape or video tape; songs

In this activity ...

Students listen to several music extracts and write down images they have as they listen.

Preparation

1. Find three to five musical pieces, preferably instrumental pieces without lyrics, that contrast in some way. Suggestions from teachers include the following:

   - Soundtrack: theme from 'Born Free'
   - Soundtrack: theme from 'Star Wars'
   - Soundtrack: theme from 'Doctor Zhivago' (Lara's Theme)
   - Beethoven: Piano concerto #5 (Emperor)
   - Ravel: Pavane for a Dead Princess
   - Debussy: The Sea (La Mer)
   - Fanshawe: African Sanctus
   - Shankar: Indian Ragas
   - Sumac: Chants of the Incas
   - Sowande: African Suite
   - Coltrane: My Favourite Things
   - Collins: Colors of the Day
   - Seeger: From a Child's Heart

2. Cue your audio tapes or compact discs at the extracts you will play for the students. Prepare to play about a one-minute extract from each piece.

In class

1. Have the students prepare a simple sheet with the titles of the extracts along the

left column and space to write several words to the right. Make the purpose of the activity clear — simply to listen to music and note down images they have as they listen.

2. Play each extract. After each extract, pause for about 30 seconds for the students to write down images they have as they listen. Encourage the students to jot down words and phrases freely, as many as come to mind. There should be no discussion and no consultation with peers at this point.

3. After the last extract is finished, ask the students to come to the blackboard (or place sheets of paper on the walls) and write their *image words* under the title of each extract.

4. Read out all of the image words to the class.

5. Play the extracts one last time.

> NOTE: *This activity is useful for promoting responsiveness in class as all student responses are equally valid. By using this activity, you can demonstrate to students that all listening — not just 'listening to language' — involves an element of appreciation and judgement.*

Variation 3.1: Similar tunes

Play two extracts that are quite similar (for example, both instrumental and by the same instrument, both from the same country, both with the same tempo). After they hear both extracts, ask the students which they prefer. Why?

Follow-up options

1. Discuss the music. *Which do you like best? Where did the extracts come from? Which would you like to listen to in your free time?*

2. Ask the students to bring in their favourite music selections. Repeat this activity or a variation of it.

Links

Consider trying activities 14.1, 19 and 37.1 as a follow-up to this activity.

Teacher's diary

How did your students do? Did all of them participate? Was any part of the activity surprising to you or your students? Would it be useful for you to elicit students' reactions and evaluations of classroom activities?

4   Personal stories

Level	Elementary and above, depending on input
Students	Young adults and adults
Purpose	Develop longer attention span for listening; promote ongoing interaction with the speaker
Text type	Teacher's prepared talk; visual aids

In this activity ...

The students listen to the teacher narrate some personal events. They ask questions for clarification and elaboration.

Preparation

1. Select some photographic slides related to your own life — your family, where you grew up, your school or university days, your travels, your hobbies. For purposes of simplifying the narration, it is best to choose several slides, with not too much visual information in any one slide. For instance, in showing slides of your family, one slide of each member individually may be better than a slide of the whole family. It is also interesting to show several slides of the same person or setting, each from a different perspective.

2. Prepare an order of presentation and one or two short remarks for each slide. Set a maximum time limit for your 'slide show', perhaps 15–20 minutes. If possible, rehearse your show. (And, of course, be sure that the slide projector works properly.)

In class

1. Begin the slide show by showing the first slide and narrating. After the first few slides, the students will probably start asking you questions spontaneously.

    Sample classroom segment

    TEACHER: *So here are some pictures of my family. This first slide (projected*

> *on to a screen or wall) is my father ... This was taken about twenty years ago, when he was in his mid-forties. Here's another slide of him. This is a more recent picture. He's 66 years old now. The next slide is a shot of Del Monte Tomato Farms. That's in central California. He worked there for 30 years.*
>
> STUDENT 1: *What was his job?*
>
> TEACHER: *He worked in the canning section.*

2. After going through the slides, ask if there are any slides anyone would like to see again. Repeat those slides only, and expand upon the narration.

NOTE: *By using personal stories, the depth of information and insight you have is virtually endless, so multiple rounds of elaboration and expansion will enrich the students' understanding. Also, by using personal stories, you will increase the students' interest, since most students do want to get to know their teachers better.*

Variation 4.1: Just narration

You can do this narration activity *without* photographs or slides, although beginning students benefit greatly from having the visual support and the structure that the 'slide show' provides. Other topics for personal stories are: frightening or dangerous experiences you've had, travel experiences, coincidences, unusual or eccentric people you have known, your earlier jobs. If possible, bring in some visual support for each personal narration you plan (such as maps or brochures for travel stories) or make a simple sketch on the blackboard to provide visual cues.

Variation 4.2: Video documentary

Prepare a voice-over documentary for some authentic video footage. Your narration can be a simplified account of the original narration from an authentic broadcast. The students take notes and later ask you questions, or answer your questions about the documentary.

Follow-up options

1. Show the slides again. Stop and ask 'quiz questions': *Do you remember who this is? Do you remember what this building is used for?* Encourage the students to *think out* their answers first, *not to call out* their answers. Then at a cue from you, they tell their answers to their partners. This technique ensures that all students have a chance to think of answers to the questions.

2. Ask the students to prepare their own 'photo' essay on a personal topic, such as 'my home town', 'what I do in my free time', 'my family tree'. Select the best essays for display or oral presentation.

Links

Consider trying activities 20 and 35 as a follow-up to this activity.

Teacher's diary

Was it difficult for you to tell 'personal stories' to your students?
What aspects of your story were the students most interested in?
What other personal stories could you use for this activity?

---

5 Questions, please!

Level	Elementary and above, depending on input
Students	All ages
Purpose	Develop quick interactions with a speaker; promote clarification exchanges
Text type	Teacher's prepared talk; stories

In this activity ...

Students ask questions in order to elicit the telling of a story or the recounting of a news article.

Preparation

1. Find an anecdote or short story that will be appealing to your students. Learn the story yourself, not by heart, but so that you can tell it well.

2. Think of several key words or phrases that will stimulate the students to ask questions to elicit the story. These are the 'story cues'.

In class

1. Tell the students that you know a story, but that they must ask you questions in order to 'elicit' the story from you.

2. Write the story cues — key words and phrases — on the blackboard. Encourage students to ask questions about these cues. (They may start simply by indicating a cue word and asking, 'What's this?')

3. When you answer the questions, you can decide to give only minimal information or to elaborate. This will depend on the willingness of the group to probe you with questions.

> NOTE: *This activity is most easily accomplished with stories having familiar rhetorical patterns, such as love stories and mystery stories. You might want to demonstrate the activity with a well-known story, such as* Romeo *and* Juliet.

Sample classroom segment

TEACHER:	(writing on the chalkboard): *Here are some phrases:* China, Great Wall, Fang, Emperor, crow, colourful fish. *These are phrases from my story. Please ask me questions to find out the story.*
STUDENT 1:	*Did the story happen in China?*
TEACHER:	*Yes. The story took place in China when the Great Wall was being built.*
STUDENT 2:	(referring to phrases on chalkboard): *Emperor? Who is the Emperor?*
TEACHER:	*The Emperor at that time was Si Wong. He was said to be very cruel. He forced all of the young, healthy men in the country to help build it.*
STUDENT 3:	*Fang? What is Fang? Is that a person?*
TEACHER:	*Yes, that's the name of a woman in the story. She was married to a man and this man was forced to go to build the Wall. She decided to go to find him since he was away from home so long.*
STUDENT 4:	*Was the Wall far from her house?*
TEACHER:	*Very far. But still she decided to ...*

(from a traditional Chinese story called 'The Faithful One')

Variation 5.1: Question pauses

Tell the story, stopping frequently to elicit questions from the students. Encourage them to ask you questions which will lead you on into the story (e.g. *What did she do after that?*) or to elaborate (e.g. *What year did the story take place?*).

Variation 5.2: Interruptions

Tell a story. Encourage the students to interrupt you to ask questions about details. For example: Teacher: *There was once a young woman who had two sisters.* Student (*interrupting*): *How old was she?* Teacher: *She was rather young, about 18 or 19 years old.*

Variation 5.3: Story boards

Children will benefit from stories most if you use vivid visual aids in the telling of your stories. Prepare some colourful background scenes (from paper or cardboard) and some eye-catching characters (attached to sticks) which you will manipulate in the scene as you tell the story. Stop frequently during the story to ask questions. Stories which lend themselves to story-board telling include: *The Three Billy Goats Gruff*,

The Gingerbread Boy, Jack and the Beanstalk, Goldilocks and the Three Bears, The Little Red Hen, The Three Little Pigs, The Riddle of the Drum.

Follow-up options

1. Try the procedure again with a different story. Once the students are familiar with this procedure, they will tend to be more inquisitive during a second story.

2. Retell the entire story, in its original scripted form. Even if it is a very literary tale in a written style, the students will be better equipped to understand it since they basically know the story from the questioning process.

3. Ask the students to write out the story in chronological order.

4. Present a script of the story with some mistakes (e.g. some character names are wrong, some events are out of sequence). Ask the students to correct the mistakes.

Links

Consider trying activities 12, 24 and 36.1 as a follow-up to this activity.

Teacher's diary

How did this activity work? Did this activity lead to a reversal of teacher and student roles (the teacher following the lead of the students)? Which of the cues helped the students to generate questions most easily? What other stories or articles could you use for this activity?

6 Who's who?

Level	Intermediate and above
Students	All ages
Purpose	Promote listening for detail; promote group interaction
Text type	Teacher's prepared instructions

In this activity ...

Students listen to directives and fill in a card to show their comprehension of the directives; as a follow-up the students guess who filled out each card.

Preparation

1. Write a list of questions to elicit personal information about the students: their occupations, background, interests, etc. You will use these questions to make directives for the upcoming task.

2. Prepare a small 'master sheet' with various shapes (lines, triangles, squares, dotted circles, solid circles, etc.) on it. Duplicate copies for the students.

3. Prepare several 'two-step directions', each involving an 'if'. By following the instructions correctly, the students will be giving clues (on their cards) about their identities. For example:

   - *Write your occupation on the card. If you are a male, write your occupation on the line in the top-left corner. If you are a female, write your name in the top-right corner. [Repeat]*
   - *What is your favourite food? Write this on the card. If you are sitting in the front of the class, write it inside the box in the middle. If you are sitting in the back of the class, write it outside the box. [Repeat]*

In class

1. Distribute one sheet to each student. Introduce the necessary vocabulary for the shapes and locations of the shapes on the sheet. Tell the students that this is a

'directions game'. They must listen very carefully to the directions. Each person's directions are different.

2. Read your 'two-step instructions', providing paraphrases and repetitions as necessary.

> NOTE: *Encourage the students to ask clarification questions if they don't understand a direction. Encourage them to be as specific as possible when asking clarification questions. For example, the question* 'Should we write our name in the right or left box?' *is a more specific clarification question than* 'Can you repeat the direction please?' *These questions are probably more useful for language learning.*

Variation 6.1: Blip!

To encourage clarification questions from the students, deliberately put in a fixed sound (a nonsense word such as 'blip' or a cough) into a direction sequence. For example, *Write your name in the 'blip'*. In order to understand the direction, the students will have to ask a question such as 'Where?' or 'Where do we write the name?' or 'Please tell us where.'

Variation 6.2: Event squares

Each student folds a sheet of paper into four squares. Each student writes one important event from his or her own life on each square. All of the students' squares are taken together and shuffled. Students take turns selecting a square and reading it aloud. The other students try to guess who wrote each event. If there are three wrong guesses, the person who wrote the square identifies himself or herself. If possible, the student who wrote the event can elaborate a bit about it before the next student selects a new event square.

Follow-up options

1. Collect the cards, shuffle them, and distribute them randomly, one to each student. Repeat the directions. Can the students guess 'who's who?'.

2. Practise filling in various kinds of authentic forms (e.g. driver's licence applications) which call for personal information. Encourage the students to work quickly, asking you for clarification of questions on the form.

Links

Consider trying activities 20.2, 28.1 and 30 as a follow-up to this activity.

Teacher's diary

Were all of the students able to participate in this activity? In what way did the students help each other in this activity? Do you think that it is beneficial for students to help each other during a listening exercise?

7   Listening skits

Level	Intermediate and above, depending on input
Students	Young adults
Purpose	Develop responsiveness to instructions; promote group interaction
Text type	Teacher's prepared instructions; drama

In this activity ...

Students perform short skits while following the directives of the 'skit director'.

Preparation

1. Compose a short skit involving three or four people. Think of a common setting, characters and situation that is familiar to your students. For example, a restaurant (setting), two customers and a waiter (characters), ordering food (situation). Visualise the situation in detail and write a chronological list of the actions and lines that each character might have in the situation. Include detailed actions (for example: *The waiter holds a pad of paper in his left hand and pencil in his right hand, as he asks in a nervous voice, 'May I take your order?'*).

2. Re-write the list as a set of specific directives. For example, *Waiter, pick up the order pad. Hold it in your left hand. Hold the pencil in your right hand. Adjust your apron. Is it on straight now? OK, now walk to the table.* Edit your list to make sure that each of the characters has an approximately equal number of actions to follow. Make sure the language is likely to be understood by your students when you say the directives.

3. Assemble any props you need for the skit. Substitute available items for authentic items — a large book for the waiter's tray, a notebook for the waiter's order pad, etc.

In class

1. Introduce the skit briefly: setting, characters, and situation. Tell the students the purpose of the activity — to listen for their directions in the skit.

2. Select students who will be the characters in the skit. For the first skits, give the more reticent students non-speaking roles. Guide the students through the skit as you give the directives.

3. Select a new group of students as characters. Guide these students through the skit, using variations in the steps (adding actions and routines, adding other lines for the characters to say).

NOTE: *Many students may become quite 'playful' during this activity. This playful attitude will help 'break the ice' in classes in which the students do not know each other well. Of course, you will still want to make sure that the students 'stay on task' — attending to directions and carrying out the skit cooperatively.*

Variation 7.1: Scenes

Select an interesting scene from a video drama. Ask the students to write out the scene as 'listening skit' directives. Use paraphrases for the characters' lines rather than trying to transcribe exactly what the speakers say. Act out the scene in the 'listening skit' format.

Follow-up options

1. Ask the students to recall the skit and to write it themselves as a set of directions or as a past tense narrative.

2. Duplicate the direction sheets for the students. Have them work in small groups to re-enact the skit, with one student in each group acting as director.

Links

Consider trying activities 9, 19.1 and 36.1 as a follow-up to this activity.

Teacher's diary

Did the students interact well with each other during the skits?
Did the students suggest their own variations for the activity? Did
the context (setting, props, predictable actions) assist the
students' comprehension?

8 Interview

Level	Elementary and above, depending on input questions
Students	Young adults and adults
Purpose	Review fixed expressions; promote fluency in interactions
Text type	Teacher's prepared questions

In this activity ...

The students are 'interviewed' individually from a set of prepared topics and questions.

Preparation

1. Think of a set of topics that you and your students can easily talk about. Families? Food? Sports? Jobs? Recent events?

2. Prepare a list of questions that you will ask the students, with a few possible variations for each question (e.g. *How many people are in your family? Do you have a large family? Could you tell me something about the size of your family?*).

3. Duplicate the list of topics and questions for the students (this may be on OHP or chalkboard, or by photocopy).

In class

1. Tell the students that you will be asking them about some of the given topics. Tell them that you will be using some of the given questions. Ask them to prepare both simple and expanded responses to the questions.

2. Call on students in a random fashion. Ask them to select one of the topics they wish to talk about. Ask the questions you have previewed, but in a different order. You may add an occasional extra question for elaboration. Be sure to ask questions for which you do not already know the answer — this increases the communicative value of the activity.

> NOTE: *If the students are capable of talking more freely, consistently ask for elaboration on each question. Also encourage the students to provide additional information without being asked for elaboration.*

Variation 8.1: Famous person

Ask each student to study some biographical facts of a famous person. When they are interviewed, the students answer as if they are that person.

Follow-up options

1. Have the students work in pairs or small groups. Repeat the procedure, with one student acting as interviewer.

2. Tape record the 'interviews'. In order to draw attention to certain grammatical forms (such as past tense) or discourse patterns (such as hesitation markers ['hmm' or 'let me think'] while you think of what to say), transcribe parts of the interviews which feature learner problems in these areas.

Links

Consider trying activities 9.2, 25 and 31 as a follow-up to this activity.

Teacher's diary

Did the activity preparation help the students to predict and answer the questions easily? Did the activity structure help them to express themselves more readily? Did the activity become repetitive? If so, what could you have done to increase the vitality of the activity?

SECTION II

INTENSIVE LISTENING

Introduction

Hearing clearly is a prerequisite for effective listening, and for practically all second-language learners, accurately perceiving the sounds in a second language is an on-going challenge. 'Hearing clearly' refers to several processes: discriminating between similar phonemes (e.g. voiced vs. voiceless consonants which have shared features, such as /t/ and /d/ and central vs. front vowels, such as /a/ and /æ/); identifying allophonic variations of the same phoneme (e.g. a flapped /t/ vs. an aspirated /t/); identifying the linguistic form when contractions, assimilations, and reductions have been used (e.g. in 'what did you do', the /t/ and /d/ sounds are assimilated and the vowel in 'you' is reduced — centralised and weakened); identifying stressed words and recognising the intonational contour of an utterance.

Focused practice in 'hearing clearly' is helpful if it comes continuously, in small doses. Some problems in perception of certain phonemic and prosodic (stress, duration, and intonation) contrasts will persist for certain learners, but your learners can and will — with sustained practice — increase their ability to perceive English sounds, words, and phrases accurately.

In addition to learning to perceive sounds clearly, **listening intensively** — in order to *appreciate the language form* of messages — is a vitally important aspect of language acquisition. In order to listen effectively and to learn the language effectively, learners need to recognise critical grammatical distinctions 'in real time' while they listen. For instance, they will need to recognise differences in verb tense, aspect, and voice (present vs. past; unmarked vs. progressive; active vs. passive) and differences between singular and plural markings of nouns and pronouns. Further, they will need to recognise the important function of stress and intonation in signalling focal elements of an utterance. This means that the learners must go beyond identifying the lexical meaning to identifying the grammatical meaning as well.

The activities in this section aim to focus learners' attention on language form in the following ways:

1. They require *attention to particular words*, phrases, grammatical units, and 'pragmatic' units (units of 'social meaning').

2. They require that the students recognise *differences* between similar words and phrases.

3. They draw *attention to sound changes* (vowel reductions and consonant assimilations) that occur in natural speech.

4. They draw attention to the speaker's use of stress, intonation, and pauses.

5. They practise *paraphrasing* (that is, having the listener restate the speaker's phrases and sentences) and *reconstructing* (that is, having the listener fill in grammatical parts that may be left out of the speaker's message).

6. They call for *remembering* specific words and sequences.

The key features of the activities in this section are the following:

- The learners work individually.
- The learners may listen as many times as they wish.

- The teacher provides feedback on accuracy.
- The teacher provides some written support.

Students at all levels of language proficiency will benefit from intensive listening activities. Beginning students may benefit from these activities most when they are used as warm-ups for activities from the attentive listening section (see Section I). Intermediate students may find these activities most useful if they are used as follow-up reviews for activities from the selective listening section (see Section III) or the interactive listening section (see Section IV). More advanced students will benefit from intensive listening activities that are targeted at particular problems of language analysis (grammar, vocabulary, or sounds) which they are working on. The nine basic activities in this section (the numerals refer to chapter numbers), along with several variations, are listed below.

9. Say it again
  Variation 9.1: Telephone game
  Variation 9.2: Add on
  Variation 9.3: Passages

10. Discrimination
  Variation 10.1: Sequence
  Variation 10.2: Odd one out

11. One-sided conversations
  Variation 11.1: Word chains

12. Alternatives
  Variation 12.1: Appropriateness
  Variation 12.2: News vocabulary
  Variation 12.3: Reduced and expanded stories
  Variation 12.4: Replacements

13. Paraphrase
   Variation 13.1: Test prep

14. Jigsaw dictation
   Variation 14.1: Pair dictation
   Variation 14.2: Fixed forms

15. Short forms
   Variation 15.1: 'Long or short?'
   Variation 15.2: Second word
   Variation 15.3: One, two, three

16. Stress
   Variation 16.1: Contrast
   Variation 16.2: Statement or question?

17. Boundaries
   Variation 17.1: Keep the pace

Many of these activities will be useful introductions to listening for beginning students in that they help the students focus their attention on simple tasks. Activities such as *Say it again, Passages, Discrimination*, and *'Long or short?'* (as well as all of the variations listed under each) can help beginning learners build up a repertoire of perception skills that will help them in more complex activities from the **Attentive Listening, Selective Listening**, and **Interactive Listening** sections. Other activities, such as *Jigsaw dictation*, can be used as a warm-up content preview, as a diagnosis of vocabulary and grammar problems, and as a means to raise awareness of lexical and grammatical form prior to other language-learning exercises.

9 Say it again

Level	Elementary and above, depending on input
Students	Young adults and adults
Purpose	Focus on phonological features; develop attention to stress and intonation
Text type	Audio tape or video tape

In this activity ...

Students watch video segments (or listen to audio-taped conversations) and repeat selected lines, attempting to imitate the exact wording, pronunciation, and intonation.

Preparation

1. Select one or more scenes from a video sequence that your students have seen (television drama, musical variety programme, commercial, feature film, etc.). The scenes you select should be of high interest to the students and have some 'memorable lines'.

> NOTE: *You may wish to have your students identify one or two scenes which* they *find particularly important, moving, memorable — and worthy of further study. In general, personal investment in the topic or scene helps students retain what they learn. This is particularly true with intensive listening exercises.*

2. List some model lines, taken directly from the tape, that you will ask the students to practise. Your list should contain only the lines, in chronological order, that you will ask the students to repeat. You need not write out the entire script of the scenes.

In class

1. Display the list of lines to be practised. Before you play the tape, ask the students to say the selected phrases or sentences. Give simple paraphrases so that the students

have a general sense of each expression. Ask if the students can recall the situations in the film in which the lines were spoken.

2. Play through the tape segment once to set the general scene. The students listen and identify where the speaker's target lines occur.

3. As you play through the tape a second time, stop *before* each 'targeted line'. The students say the line as you point to it on the blackboard, first all together and then individually. After a few repetitions, continue the segment. Stop the tape again after the line and elicit additional repetitions. Encourage the students to feel as if they are 'saying the line' (as a character with a specific motive), not simply 'repeating the line' (for language practice).

Variation 9.1: Telephone game

Send a verbal message around the room. Tell a short message to one student. That student whispers it to another student, and so on, until every student has tried to hear the message clearly and to repeat it accurately. Compare the final version with your original message.

Variation 9.2: Add on

Start with a simple sentence that can allow for 'add-ons'. A common example is: I went to the supermarket yesterday and bought (*should have bought, wanted to buy . . . but I forgot to*) some milk . . . some bananas . . . a pound of cheese. The students work in groups, with each student repeating the previous sentence before adding on a new part. How many add-ons can they make and still remember the whole sentence?

Variation 9.3: Passages

Select some short passages — prose or poetry or songs — which are especially well-written and memorable. Passages which evoke visual imagery are especially good. Record the passages on individual audio tapes (with musical background if you wish). These will be take-home tapes for the students. Tell the students to follow these steps: first, read the text to yourself as you listen to the tape. Second, read the passage silently to yourself. Third, follow again as you listen to the tape. Fourth, put the written text away. Listen to the tape only several times during the day. The students will usually come to memorise the passages in this way.

Follow-up options

1. Write out some of the lines on the blackboard. Mark the stressed syllables with

a heavy accent mark. Using your finger on a table, tap out a rhythm as you say the line. Ask your students to try to say the line in this rhythm.

2. To make the lines more memorable, ask some students to draw a simple sketch — a 'still shot' — of the scene with the caption below the scene (or in speech bubbles next to the characters).

Links

Consider trying activities 29 and 36.2 as a follow-up to this activity.

Teacher's diary

Did you model the lines for the students or were they able to use the video tape as the model? Were the students 'saying the lines' or simply 'repeating the lines'? What other sources can you use for this kind of activity?

---

10 Discrimination

Level	Elementary
Students	All ages
Purpose	Identify vocabulary items
Text type	Text read aloud; description

In this activity . . .

Students listen to brief statements and point to the visual display (picture, graph, words) corresponding to the vocabulary items they hear.

Preparation

1. Prepare an audio tape, or speaking notes, which include a related set of vocabulary items that your students will need to recognise.

2. Prepare a 'visuals sheet'. This sheet will contain related lexical items — either illustrations or verbal expressions. Place a number under each picture or item.

> NOTE: *Some commercially available 'picture boards', such as 'Uni-Sets', which contain cardboard settings (of country maps, airports, houses, towns, playgrounds, markets, classrooms, etc.) and vinyl cut-outs of people and objects, can be very useful for this kind of activity, particularly in small classes. You may also find it useful to collect small cut-out pictures from magazines to create your own picture vocabulary sets.*

In class

1. Distribute the visuals sheet to the students. Ask them to 'read' the sheet. If the sheet consists of visuals, ask them for how many they know the English words. If the sheet consists of words, ask them to pronounce the items.

2. Play the tape or 'read the script' (using your notes). Students point at the correct part of the visual as you go through the sequence, and say, 'now point to the . . . '.

NOTE: *By having the students point, rather than tick or circle or number the correct items, you can use the same visuals repeatedly, with differing information 'input' each time.*

Sample tape script

(Based on a house diagram)

Here's the floor plan for a typical house that you might find in the United States. We're going to go through the house, starting at the front. So walking up to the front door, that's the walkway. Everybody, point to the walkway. (Teacher walks around to be sure that they have identified it.) Now, the walkway leads to the front door. Please point to the front door ...

Variation 10.1: Sequence

Say several of the items in sequence, either saying just the words, or in phrases. Students listen and number the pictures in the order you said them (or draw arrows to indicate the sequence). This exercise helps to build the students' aural memory.

Variation 10.2: Odd one out

Place three or four of the vocabulary items in a line:

   cottage   tent   cliff   cabin

Ask questions which will make the students discriminate between the items. For example, *Which of these is not a place to live? Which of them can you carry with you? Which one doesn't begin with a /k/ sound?* By using multiple ways to think about vocabulary items, the students are more likely to remember them.

Follow-up options

1. Vocabulary quiz. Give a description of the items. The students write down the target words.

2. Vocabulary notebook. Allow time for the students to enter the new words into a vocabulary notebook that they keep for review.

Links

Consider trying activities 14.1, 14.2 and 21.2 as a follow-up to this activity.

Teacher's diary

How well did the activity go? What parts of the activity did your students find useful? Do your students think discrimination practice is important for listening development?

11   One-sided conversations

Level   Intermediate and above, depending on input

Students   Young adults and adults

Purpose   Identify grammatical features and discourse links; develop
                    inferencing ability

Text type   Audio tape; telephone conversations

In this activity ...

Students listen to one side of a telephone conversation and work out what the other
speaker is saying.

Preparation

1. Find, or compose, some telephone conversations in which both parties talk for
    about the same amount of time.

    Sample tape segment

    Telephone conversation

    Hi, Dad. This is Cheryl.

    . . .

    Fine, just fine. Listen, I'm sorry to call so late.

    . . .

    Oh, good. Listen, I just wanted to call you to thank you for the birthday present.

    . . .

    Yes, it fits just fine.

    . . .

2. Prepare a one-sided script, with blank lines for the unknown speaker.

In class

1. Give the class some general background for the activity without saying too much
    about the content of each conversation. Play the whole sequence once. Can they

figure out the topics of the conversation? Write the topics on the blackboard as they tell them to you.

2. On second playing of the tape, stop after some of the lines and ask: *What did the other speaker say?* Students should write their responses rather than call them out, in order that all have an opportunity to respond.

3. Play through the conversation a third time, asking the students to confirm what they have written.

4. Distribute the tape script. Ask the students to identify the links between the known speaker's lines and the lines they wrote for the unknown speaker. Are the connections only between the immediately surrounding lines? Or are some of the connections across several lines?

Sample student paper (completed)

Telephone conversation

Hi, Dad. This is Cheryl.
Hello, Cheryl. It's good to hear from you. How are you?

Fine, just fine. Listen, I'm sorry to call so late.
No problem. I'm always up until about midnight.

Oh, good. Listen, I just wanted to call you to thank you for the birthday present.
You're welcome. I knew you wanted a sweater, but I couldn't remember your size. Does it fit?

Yes, it fits just fine.

Variation 11.1: Word chains

Ask the students to identify a chain of words that provide 'cohesion' links for the conversation. For example. This is *Cheryl*. Oh, hi, *Cheryl*. [Cohesion link = repeating her name.] I'm calling to *thank you* for the *sweater*. Oh, *you're welcome*. [Cohesion link = a kind of 'social formula' — 'Thank you' and 'You're welcome'.] Does *it* fit? [Cohesion link = a noun and a pronoun reference: *the sweater, it*.] This exercise does *not* need to become exhaustive — the students do not have to find *all* the possible links. Simply having the students identify one set of links per conversation will help raise their attention to cohesion markers as they listen.

Follow-up options

1. List different answers the students gave for the unknown speaker. Discuss which are possible and why.

2. Ask the students to tape-record one of their own telephone conversations, from their side only. Listen to the tape recordings of these conversations in class.

3. Role play: the teacher plays one side of a telephone conversation; individual students play the other side. Introduce various situations and reasons for calling.

Links

Consider trying activities 25.1 and 33.2 as a follow-up to this activity.

Teacher's diary

What parts of the activity did the students find difficult? What help did the students ask for?

---

12 Alternatives

Level	Intermediate and above, depending on input
Students	Young adults and adults
Purpose	Compare different words and grammatical forms
Text type	Text read aloud; narrative or expository

In this activity . . .

Students listen to two spoken texts, which have slight differences between them. The students identify the differences.

Preparation

1. Identify a text that will be interesting to your students and challenging for them to understand. Prepare an alternative version of the text, with small changes in vocabulary or syntax.

2. Record both versions of the text. Prepare a transcript for the original, unaltered version.

In class

1. Provide some background for the text. Ask the students to relax as they listen. Read the text through twice at a slightly slower than normal pace so that the students can understand the general meaning of it.

2. Distribute the transcript of the original version. Read the text again, using the alternative version, which will have several differences. Ask the students to circle places in the text that are different.

Sample texts

(i) Never drink lemon tea from a polystyrene cup because the chemical combination of tea and lemon dissolves the material of the container. This discovery was made by Dr Michael Philips of the Connecticut Health Center in 1985, but most tea

drinkers are not aware of it. Dr Philips advises tea drinkers to use bone china cups, since it is suspected that soluble polystyrene may cause cancer.

(ii) You should not drink lemon tea from a Styrofoam cup because the chemical combination of tea and lemon dissolves the material of the container. This fact was discovered by Dr Michael Philips of the Connecticut Health Center in 1985, but most tea drinkers are not aware of it. Dr Philips advises tea drinkers that they should use bone china cups, since it is known that polystyrene, in its soluble form, may cause cancer.

From *New England Journal of Medicine*.

Variation 12.1: Appropriateness

Prepare two versions of a conversation involving functions such as requests or apologies. Ask the students to identify how the conversations differ. (For example: in version 1 a teenage sister, Ann, and her brother, Bill, are sitting at a table, doing their homework. Ann: 'Could you give me that pen?' Bill: 'Yeah. Here.' In version 2 Ann is at a bank counter the next day, talking to the bank clerk. Ann: 'Would you mind if I borrow your pen?' Clerk: 'No, not at all. Here you are.') Most students will be able to identify the general differences between the conversations (informal vs. formal). Encourage them to identify the specific differences in wording and intonation.

Variation 12.2: News vocabulary

Prepare a list of vocabulary items (words or phrases) that occur in a news broadcast. For each one, provide a similar expression:

> *believed to have kidnapped / believed to have taken*
> *returned the baby / brought back the baby*
> *surrendered to the police / gave herself up to the police*

Students listen to the broadcast and identify which of the two terms was actually used. This may lead to a short discussion or explanation of the different nuances of the terms.

Sample tape segment

> *A woman who is believed to have kidnapped a 3-month-old boy on Wednesday returned the baby and surrendered to the police on Sunday. Police quoted Kazuko Sudana as saying that on Sunday she had won a stroller in a company lottery and had been asked to submit a picture of herself with her baby in the stroller. Since Sudana was childless, she said that she had only intended 'to borrow' the baby in order to allow her boss to continue believing that Sudana was the mother of four children.*

Variation 12.3: Reduced and expanded stories

Students read a reduced version of a story and then hear an expanded version of the story, read to them by the teacher. Students raise their hands when they recognise an addition to the story.

Variation 12.4: Replacements

Distribute copies of a news article to the students a day in advance of this listening activity. Prepare an alternative version of the story or article, in which you change several lexical expressions. Some of the lexical changes should be roughly equivalent in meaning, while some of the lexical changes should alter the meaning significantly. Overall, the two versions should be fairly close in meaning. Play the recorded version. Ask the students to identify changes in the story, then to show which changes altered the meaning of the story.

Links

Consider trying activities 28 and 35 as a follow-up to this activity.

Teacher's diary

What did your students do to notice the differences in the passages? What kinds of differences were easiest for them to notice? How many differences can one person notice at a time?

---

13 Paraphrase

Level	Intermediate and advanced
Student	Adults
Purpose	Identify meaning from fast, natural speech when contractions, assimilations and reductions are used; develop aural memory
Text type	Audio tape; conversations

In this activity ...

Students are presented with various lines from a passage and are asked to provide paraphrases.

Preparation

1. Select an audio-taped or video-taped selection that the students are already familiar with — perhaps an extract that you have used in a selective listening activity. Identify some 'target lines' which, out of context, would be ambiguous or not very explicit in their meaning.

2. Prepare a list of the 'target lines'. You may also prepare some multiple-choice paraphrases for each line.

   Sample tape segment

   A: How long have you been married?
   B: Just five years. We had our anniversary last week. How about you? You're married too, aren't you?
   A: Yes, I am.
   B: How long have you been married?
   A: Gee, I don't know. Let me see. I guess about 11 or 12 years. To tell the truth, I can't remember our wedding date any more.
   B: You can't remember?
   A: **Don't tell my husband that, though.** *[< a target line]*

[Possible paraphrase: She said, 'Don't tell my husband that I can't remember our wedding date.' She means that her husband might be upset if he knows that she can't remember it.]

In class

1. Tell the class that you are going to practise paraphrasing (and also 'reported speech'). Give some examples, using classroom language. For example, if you say, 'Danielle, please open the window', a student might say in *reported speech* that 'you asked Danielle to open the window'. A student might say in paraphrase that 'you wanted some air in the room'. Paraphrase usually involves some 'inferencing', or filling in reasons.

2. Remind the students of the situation on the tape. Write the target line on the blackboard.

3. Play the segment in which the line appears. Ask the students to paraphrase the line. Encourage them to try to be specific about what the speaker means.

> NOTE: *Listen for the* meaning *of the students' paraphrases. It is probably best for this activity not to correct the students' grammar and vocabulary at this point, provided that you can understand what the students mean.*

Variation 13.1: Test prep

Write out several single sentences that you will record on audio tape. For each sentence prepare three paraphrase choices, only one of which is a correct paraphrase (from a strict vocabulary or grammatical viewpoint). For example:

(on tape)
She said I'd better not go there.

(written paraphrases)
(a) She told me that she wouldn't go.
(b) She told me a better place to go.
(c) She told me that I shouldn't go.

To correct the exercise, it may be most useful for the students themselves to figure out the right answers. In this way, they will become more directly involved in the analysis of the grammar and vocabulary points.

Links

Consider trying activities 26.1 and 30.1 as a follow-up to this activity.

Teacher's diary

Which target lines were difficult to paraphrase? What kinds of difficulties did they have? In what kinds of ways can you work with the students on this kind of language difficulty?

14 Jigsaw dictation

Level	Elementary and above, depending on input
Students	Young adults and adults
Purpose	Raise awareness of grammatical features and grammatical categories
Text type	Text read aloud

In this activity ...

The students listen to a passage and take dictation. Students work in pairs, with one member of each pair knowing some of the wording of the passage.

Preparation

1. Select a high-interest passage that will be of value for the students to use for further study. Literary and semi-literary passages may be suitable: haiku, other poems, excerpts from novels, plays, short stories, famous speeches, specially constructed paragraphs, riddles.

    Sample text

    > *Solitude*
    >
    > *There now, where the first crumb*
    > *Falls from the table*
    > *You think no one hears it*
    > *As it hits the floor*
    >
    > *. . .*
    >
    > (Charles Simic)

2. Make two gapped versions of the text. In each of these versions, provide gaps for all the words of one grammatical category (such as nouns or verbs or articles).

67

A.

Solitude

There now, where the first crumb

_____ *from the table*
You _____ *no one* _____ *it*
As it _____ *the floor*

B.

_____

There now, from where _____
_____ _____
Falls from _____ _____
_____ *think* _____ *hears* _____
As _____ *hits* _____ _____

NOTE: *Dictation is a standard technique for* testing *students' ability at recognising words and grammatical stuctures. For* teaching *purposes, it is best to make the dictation formats varied and to keep them focused on particular teaching points. Remember that if the students are asked to write too much, the activity is likely to become tedious and lose its learning focus.*

In class

1. Read the passage once aloud. Be sure that the students have a general understanding of the text.

2. Arrange the students in A—B pairs. Distribute one of the gapped texts to the A students, the other to the B students.

3. Read the text again. Provide longer than usual pauses between sense groups of words so that the students have time to write, but use natural phrasing as you read.

4. Have the A—B partners consult with each other to arrive at the full text. It is best if they do this orally, without simply showing each other their versions.

5. Finally, read the entire passage again.

Variation 14.1: Pair dictation

Provide each member of the student pairs with half of the text. The students dictate their parts to each other in order to complete the text.

Variation 14.2: Fixed forms

Dictate a short passage. Ask the students to write down *only* the members of a fixed grammatical class — nouns or adjectives or verbs or adverbs or articles. (You may wish to assign different students different forms. In this way, they can try to assemble the passage from the bits each student has written down.)

Follow-up options

1. Discuss the texts you used in the activity. What do you think the writer is like? What is the writer's viewpoint? How did the writer feel at the time of writing the text?

2. Have your students look through anthologies of poems that you bring to class. Ask them to choose poems to use for oral readings.

Links

Consider trying activities 21.1 and 36.1 as a follow-up to this activity.

Teacher's diary

Was this activity engaging for the students? Can you think of stimulating sources for this activity? Do you know of other ideas for using dictation?

---

15 Short forms

Level	Elementary and intermediate
Students	Young adults and adults
Purpose	Improve aural discrimination; identify meaning from fast, natural speech when assimilations are used; appreciate that many individual phonemes in English have variant pronunciations (allophones)
Text type	Teacher's prepared presentation

In this activity . . .

Students practise identifying 'short forms' of words in connected speech.

Preparation

1. Identify some common 'short forms' that your students have trouble hearing in rapid speech. ('Short forms' is used here to mean any kind of sound change that is brought about by stress timing in connected speech.) Common examples are:

    (a) Weakened grammatical words in question form:
    Have you eaten yet? [hævju]
    Did she see it? [dıči]
    Are they still there? [aðei]
    Is it finished? [zit]
    (b) Assimilated consonant clusters:
    Ha*nd b*ag becomes [hæmbæg]
    going to becomes [gʊnə]
    ni*ce sh*ape becomes [naišeip]
    (c) Reductions of vowels:
    America becomes [amerəkə]
    movement becomes [mʊvmənt]

    If possible, choose examples directly from passages (broadcasts and conversations) that the students have just listened to in other listening exercises.

2. List the syllables in a vertical format.

have	did	hand	go-	move-	A-
you	she	bag	ing	ment	me-
eat-	see		to		ri-
en	it				ca
yet					

In class

1. Display the vertical format of the words and phrases. Pronounce the words (or syllables) in isolation with clear pauses beween them.

2. Then pronounce the words in a normal 'connected' style. Ask the students to identify which part has changed.

Variation 15.1: 'Long or short?'

Read the target forms. The students try to identify whether the form is spoken in connected speech style, with normal assimilations ('short' / 'connected'), or whether you are artificially articulating each word clearly ('long' / 'unconnected'). This exercise will help draw the students' attention to the range of 'weak' pronunciations for unstressed parts of a phrase.

Variation 15.2: Second word

Ask the students to write down the second (or third) word in sentences which have weak (reduced stress) forms. Examples: *He's got a cold today. He's in his room. His fever has gone down a bit. He'll be back to work tomorrow.* This exercise will help draw the students' attention to the role of grammar knowledge in listening.

Variation 15.3: One, two, three

Write down the stressed words of an utterance. For example, words in bold in the following sentences are usually stressed: '**Where** did you **go** last **Friday**?' I **went** to **visit** a **friend**. Write the stressed words in a random order on the blackboard:

go	**Friday**	**where**
friend	**visit**	**went**

Say the sentences with normal stress and intonation. Ask the students to mark the words in the order — one, two, three — that they occurred. After they do this, ask them to try to recall the exact sentences. This exercise will help the students realise that attention to stressed words is most important in remembering what was said.

Follow-up options

1. Ask the students to keep notes over a period of a week of any English expressions they find hard to understand when spoken, but easy to understand when written. Write these on the blackboard and see if the students can identify the 'sound change rules' (assimilations, elisions, vowel reductions) that occur when the words are spoken.

2. Discuss the role of 'short forms' in language comprehension and in language production. Point out to the students that it is *not* essential for students to try to use reduced and assimilated forms in their own speech. Point out that these 'short forms' are the result of the speaker giving greater stress to some syllables and thereby less stress to others. Encourage the students to improve their pronunciation and fluency by focusing on appropriate stress, not on trying to mimic short forms.

Links

Consider trying activities 3 and 21.2 as a follow-up to this activity.

Teacher's diary

How well did the activity go? Did any of your students show special interest in this activity? What do you find to be the most effective length of time for this type of intensive listening activity?

---

16 Stress

Level	Elementary
Students	Young adults and adults
Purpose	Develop aural discrimination; develop awareness of functions of stress and intonation
Text type	Teacher's prepared presentation

In this activity ...

Students listen to sentences and identify the stressed syllables and words.

Preparation

1. Write a series of question and answer exchanges in which different content words can be stressed to create a contrast of emphasis. For example:

    Exchange 1:
    Is the **man** in the green car your friend?
    No, the **woman** in the green car is my friend.

    Exchange 2:
    Is the man in the **green** car your friend?
    No, the man in the **red** car is my friend.

    Exchange 3:
    Is the man in the green **car** your friend?
    No, the man on the green **motocycle** is my friend.

    Exchange 4:
    Is the man in the green car your friend?
    No, the man in the green car **is not** my friend.

2. Write the sentences out on the blackboard, without indicating any stress on any words, or write the sentences out on cards, with one word on each card.

3. You may wish to sketch a simple visual for each question and answer pair to establish a possible context for each exchange.

In class

1. Read each exchange with the appropriate stress.

2. Ask the students to identify which word was most stressed in each speaker's line.

Follow-up options

1. Read the first line of each exchange, giving stress to one of the items. Ask individual students to respond.

2. Provide illustrations in which contrasting sentences are possible. Any picture with two possibly confusable items or persons will serve the purpose (for example, a picture of two cups on a table, a black cup and a white cup). Ask the students to write out, then say, different exchanges to show the contrast of stress. For example, 'Is the **black** cup yours?' 'No, the **white** cup is mine'.

Variation 16.1: Contrast

Read aloud a statement or a question. Ask the students to identify whether it has 'normal' or 'unusual' stress. For example, 'Where do you want to **go** tonight?' (with 'go' stressed) is 'normal', while 'Where do **you** want to go tonight?' (with 'you' stressed) is 'unusual', or not the typical stress. Ask the students what the 'unusual' stress might mean: can you think of a situation in which this stress makes sense? For example, if someone has just asked you where you would like to go, and you return the question, 'Where do **you** want to go tonight?' 'you' would be a suitable stress.

Variation 16.2: Statement or question?

Read aloud some statements that could be either declarative statements or questions depending on the sentence's final intonation: for example, 'I should come to class on Sunday?' vs. 'I should come to class on Sunday'. The first sentence would have rising intonation to indicate a question — in most varieties of English. The second sentence would have falling intonation to indicate a declarative statement of fact. After you read each sentence, ask the students to say 'Statement' or 'Question'.

Links

Consider trying activities 20 and 36.2 as a follow-up to this activity.

Teacher's diary

Did the students find anything surprising in this lesson? Can you think of ways to increase their awareness of stress and intonation in conversation activities?

17 Boundaries

Level	Elementary and intermediate
Students	Young adults, adults
Purpose	Develop aural discrimination; develop awareness of tone groups (pause groups) as units for processing spoken language
Text type	Teacher's prepared presentation

In this activity ...

Students listen to utterances and mark the pause boundaries.

Preparation

1. Make some transcripts of tape-recorded monologues or dialogues. You may wish to make your own recordings of short monologues for this activity, or you may use naturally occurring conversation. (However, if you use dialogues, there should be very little speaker overlap in the samples you select.)

2. Before doing this activity with your class, rehearse your reading, or listen to the recordings and check them with the transcript. As you rehearse (or listen), place slash marks (/) in the transcript after each clear pause. (You may wish to use a double slash to indicate longer pauses.)

Sample passage

Last night/I was on my way/to the pub/when I ran across/an old friend/named Michael//He was with someone/I had never seen before//The man he was with/was wearing a dark raincoat/and had his hands/in his pockets//It seemed strange to me/that the man/was walking behind Michael/rather than at his side//I asked Michael/if he wanted to come along with me//Michael gave me an uncomfortable look/and rolled his eyes/toward the man behind him//Then I realised that . . .

In class

1. Distribute the transcripts without the pause markers written in.

2. Read the text and have the students place a slash mark (/) in the text where they hear a pause.

Follow-up options

1. Have the students practise reading the text in appropriate pause groups.

2. Read the passage yourself with *in*appropriate pause boundaries. Ask the students what effect this has on their comprehension. (Inappropriate pause boundaries should seriously interfere with understanding!)

Variation 17.1: Keep the pace

Read aloud a short monologue passage. (You should mark your copy for intended pauses in advance.) The first time through have the students indicate the pauses with slash marks (/). The second time through the passage, have the students follow the pace of your reading with their fingers. Can they notice differences of pacing? The third time ask them to mark each 'pause group' for 'pace' — fast, medium, or slow pace. They can use marks such as +, −, 0 for the three labels. After you finish, ask them to identify patterns. Which segments were fast? (Usually 'given information' that the listener already knows, or 'asides' that aren't so important, tend to be uttered more quickly.) Which segments were somewhat slow? (Usually, pause groups with 'new information' are uttered a bit more slowly.) Which segments have a *very* slow pace? (Usually, segments that require a lot of thought or careful word selection, or segments that are especially emphasised may be said quite slowly.)

Links

Consider trying activity 25.1 as a follow-up.

Teacher's diary

What did the students find valuable about this lesson? What did the students want to practise more?

SECTION III

SELECTIVE LISTENING

Introduction

Selective listening activities address two separate, yet equally important, goals in language development. The first goal concerns listening as an active process of predicting information and then selecting 'cues' that surround this information; the second goal concerns becoming familiar with the organisation of different types of discourse.

Because listening is an active process, it goes without saying that learners have to participate actively in order to improve their listening ability. Learners can experience how their listening ability is developing when they have opportunities to test the *consequences* of their attempts to listen. This means that to evaluate how well they have understood, learners need to develop their own goals for listening and to evaluate their efforts at reaching these goals.

Because development of listening ability involves increasing our learners' access to different kinds of listening situations, it is important for us to expose our learners to a range of authentic types of spoken language. However, since most of our learners will *initially* find authentic listening rather frustrating, we can introduce them to authentic language through *selective listening tasks*. Selective listening tasks focus the learners' attention on *key parts* of the discourse. By noticing key parts of the discourse, the learners can build up their understanding of the overall meaning by inferring, or 'filling in', what they have missed.

The activities in this section are designed to address both of these purposes. The activities aim to develop students' listening ability in three ways:

1. By promoting attempts to listen to a range of authentic spoken language (that is, to a range of speakers, topics, and situations).

2. By focusing expectations on understanding the main ideas of a text and on completing a specific task.

3. By providing pre-listening work which helps the learner understand the overall function and organisation of the listening extract.

The **key features** of the activities in this section are:

- The learners focus on selected information as they listen.
- The learners have the opportunity for a second listening to check their understanding.

- The teacher makes frequent use of taped materials.
- The teacher provides warm-up activities prior to listening.
- The teacher helps students set a purpose before listening.
- The teacher requires *minimal use of written language* during the activity.
- The teacher gives immediate feedback following the activity.

There are twelve basic activity outlines in this section. Once again, with each activity there are suggestions for variations in which the learners can work toward the same instructional goals.

18. Cues game
   Variation 18.1: Teams

19. Sound sequences
   Variation 19.1: Sound skit
   Variation 19.2: Sound bingo
   Variation 19.3: Sound track

20. That's not right!
   Variation 20.1: Memory game
   Variation 20.2: Contradiction game

21. Images
   Variation 21.1: Listen for this!
   Variation 21.2: Elicit the words

22. Recorded messages
   Variation 22.1: Service encounters

23. Facts and figures
   Variation 23.1: Documentary

24. Story maps
   Variation 24.1: Predict the next part
   Variation 24.2: Argument map

25. Talk show
   Variation 25.1: Whose line?
   Variation 25.2: Opinion gap

26. In order
   Variation 26.1: Monologues

27. Topic listening
   Variation 27.1: Write your questions
   Variation 27.2: Standard questions

28. Conversation clues
Variation 28.1: Which was it?
Variation 28.2: Test questions

29. Episode
Variation 29.1: Self-access

Some of the activities in this section, particularly *Cues game*, *Sound sequences*, *That's not right!* and *In order*, will be enjoyable for most learners because of their game-like format. However, as they play these games, the learners are very much practising selective listening.

Other activities, most notably *Recorded messages* and *Facts and figures*, have a more 'serious' character to them in that they are primarily information-gathering tasks. Nevertheless, these activities too are intended to generate a high level of learner involvement. There are several 'real-world links' for the activities in this section:

- listening to announcements for specific information
- listening to news reports to update your knowledge of a situation
- listening to speeches or lectures
- listening to recorded messages to note important information
- listening to stories to understand the main points
- listening to songs for appreciation of the lyrics
- listening for specific information in service encounters

When you are doing the activities in this section, it is helpful to point out to the learners these important links. When possible, provide introductory or follow-up activities that actually utilise 'real world' discourse samples.

Another point to note concerns promoting listening practice outside the classroom. Since many, if not most, students will have access to sources of spoken English outside the classroom, particularly English-language media (television, video films, radio), and will be motivated to take advantage of these sources, it is sensible to develop a link between classroom learning and out-of-class learning.

The last part of this section on selective listening, which is a variation of the activity called *Episode*, is entitled *Self-access*. Consider ways in which you might help your learners set up and maintain a self-access listening programme. Most learners will appreciate knowing how to get more out of self-access listening opportunities. By providing standard listening guides, which are usable for different types of recorded materials, and by organising report forms, you can assist your students in developing listening and learning skills.

18 Cues game

Level	Elementary and above, depending on input
Students	Children and young adults
Purpose	Develop inferencing skill; use known words and ideas to infer missing information
Text type	Teacher's prepared question cues

In this activity ...

The students listen to cues and try to guess the target word. This activity helps the students build up their inferencing skills in English.

Preparation

1. Select a theme such as *countries*, *export products*, *machines*, *famous people*, *sports*, *exotic foods*, *emotions*, *colours*. Make a list of related vocabulary items, and some cues for each vocabulary item. The cues need not be complete sentences.

2. Order your cues. Keep the cues which might give away the answer until last. For example, if the theme is 'animals' and the target word is 'elephant', order your cues as follows: *is found in Africa, is an endangered species, is large, runs slowly, has thick skin, has ivory tusks.*

In class

1. Set the theme for the game. If you have prepared several topic areas, let the students select the topic they want.

2. Read the cues, pausing after each one to allow for guessing.

Variation 18.1: Teams

This can be played as a 'cooperative learning' endeavour in a team format, with one cue offered at a time to each team. Points are awarded based on the number of cues required to make a correct guess.

Follow-up options

1. Present some vocabulary items to the students, working in groups. Ask them to write 'cues' for the next game.

2. Present an unordered list of cues for each of the vocabulary items you used. Ask the students to order the cues according to some criterion, such as how obvious the cue is.

Links

Consider trying activities 6.1, 12.4 and 31.1 as a follow-up to this activity.

Teacher's diary

Did the game format stimulate the students to participate more than they usually do? How would you revise this activity in order to help the students guess more often or more quickly?

19 Sound sequences

Level	Intermediate
Students	All ages
Purpose	Develop inferencing ability; develop use of background knowledge to fill in missing information
Text type	Audio tape; sound effects

In this activity ...

Students listen to a sequence of two to four sounds (e.g. sound of footsteps, a package falling to the ground, someone singing a tune), only one of which has words in it. The students try to imagine a setting and characters that fit the sounds. This activity helps the students build up visualisation skills for listening to English.

Preparation

1. Prepare a dubbed tape of various sequences of sound effects (e.g. *footsteps*, *door opening*, *tap water running*).

2. Prepare some empty cartoon strips, with one square for each step in each sequence. Provide a few visual cues in the squares.

   Sample tape segment

   1. Elevator door opening: *'Oh, it's you'* (with surprise or with disappointment).

   2. Cat meowing, vase breaking: *'I'm so sorry'* (sincerely or sarcastically).

In class

1. Distribute the cartoon strips. Explain the purpose of the activity: to make a possible story from the sounds. Play the tape and have the students, individually or in pairs, complete each sequence, using simple line drawings.

2. After playing several sequences, and noting the differences among the students' drawings, go back to the first one. Replay the sequence. Ask questions to bring

out the different interpretations: *Is the speaker a man or a woman? About how old is he or she? What is the setting? Is this in an office building? In an apartment house? What did she see when the elevator doors opened?* Emphasise that the different interpretations are valid if they are based on the actual cues.

Variation 19.1: Sound skit

Ask two or three students to prepare a 'sound skit' (with voices and sound effects) that they can perform in the classroom. Other students close their eyes (put their heads down or face the back of the room) while the skit is performed. Which of the listeners can reconstruct the scene (including remembering whose voice said which lines)?

Variation 19.2: Sound bingo

If you have compiled a large number of sound effects, you can play a game (usually popular among children) in which learners have grids with differing patterns of pictures representing different sounds (e.g. shoes representing the sound of footsteps). As they hear a sound, they cover the picture on their grid with a marker. The first person to cover all of the pictures or a line of them wins.

Variation 19.3: Sound track

Play a recording of the sound track from a scene in a film. Ask the students to list the sights that will be in the picture: characters (age, physical appearance, posture, clothing, distance between characters) and setting (surrounding view, visible objects). Compile the lists by having the students write their guesses on the blackboard. Now watch the video portion of the scene (with or without the sound). What parts of the scene were easy to predict? What parts of the scene was no one able to predict?

Follow-up options

1. Let students prepare their own recordings of sound sequences. For each sequence, they must prepare a cartoon strip which is the 'correct' answer. The other students try to put the pictures in order as they listen.

2. Ask the students to write short stories, using one of the sound sequences as the initial setting for the story.

3. Have members of the class go on expeditions to specific sites to record sounds: train stations, supermarkets, restaurants. What sounds can be heard?

Links

Consider trying activities 3, 7.1, 30.1 and 36.2 as a follow-up to this activity.

Teacher's diary

Which of the variations and follow-up options did you try? Which did you avoid? Why?

20 That's not right!

Level	Elementary
Students	All ages
Purpose	Develop ability to identify inconsistency and contradiction in information heard
Text type	Teacher's prepared presentation; visual aids

In this activity ...

Students look at a picture as they listen to a description. They verify the statements by saying 'that's right!' or 'that's not right!'

Preparation

1. Find a picture (photograph or illustration) that is large enough for all the students to see, or make copies for individuals or small groups. Use a picture that contains vocabulary items that you wish the students to learn.

2. Prepare a list of statements about the picture, some true and some false. Start with statements that are very simple. Gradually introduce compound sentences (with use of 'and', 'or', 'but') which are more difficult to verify.

In class

1. Place the photograph in a position where it can be seen easily. If the students are unfamiliar with vocabulary items, you may initially describe the picture while pointing to various parts of it. Tell the students you will make several statements about the picture — some true, some false (and, if you wish, some which can't be verified from the picture).

2. Read your statements with normal intonation and speed. You may wish to number your statements so that all students can write down 'true' or 'false' (or 'maybe') after each statement. Alternatively, students can call out 'that's right' or 'that's not right' following each statement.

Sample segment

(Based on an illustration of a service department at a large appliance store)

1. There are two women in this picture. 2. One of them is holding something.
3. She's holding a telephone. 4. She's holding a telephone answering machine.
5. The sign on the wall says 'Customer Service Department'. 6. Both of these
people work for the store.

Variation 20.1: Memory game

This can be done as a memory game, with the students first seeing the photograph
and then having it removed. When the statements are read they have to recall the
scene, as well as understand the statement. Encourage the students to actually visualise
the scene as they listen to your statements.

Variation 20.2: Contradiction game

Done without pictures, this game calls for the students to listen and identify contradictions in an account. Rather than say 'that's right' or 'that's not right', the students
say, 'that doesn't make sense' when they hear a contradiction. For example: *I woke*
up this morning about 7:30 and had a quick shower and a cup of coffee. Then I ran
out of the house and was lucky enough to catch the 7:15 bus. (Students should interrupt:
That doesn't make sense — you couldn't catch the 7:15 bus if you woke up at 7:30.)
Then, I got off the bus in front of my home . . . It is best to start with several scenes
(such as the 'getting to work' scene above) that can be visualised by the students.

Follow-up options

1. True or false? Ask the students to write five statements about themselves, some
    true and some false. (For example: *I was born in 1972. I worked one summer*
    on a fishing boat.) Each student reads his or her statements. Other students try
    to guess which are true and which are false.

2. The students work in pairs or small groups. Provide each group with a large
    photograph. Each group writes ten statements — 4 true, 4 false, and 2 'no
    information available'. Then each group holds up its picture as it reads its
    statements. Other students answer.

3. Assemble several similar photographs. Ask the students to write short paragraphs
    describing one or more of the photos. Jumble the photos and descriptions and
    ask the students to match them.

Links

Consider trying activities 5, 10.1, 34 and 34.2 as a follow-up to this activity.

Teacher's diary

How did your students do in this activity? What other language learning activities can you construct using photographs?

---

21 Images

Level	Intermediate and above, depending on input
Students	Young adults and adults
Purpose	Develop ability to listen for gist, focus on overall meaning
Text type	Audio tape; songs

In this activity ...

The students listen several times to a song. They recall key words and relate groups of words to impressions they have from the song.

Preparation

Select one song or two songs by the same song writer. The lyrics should communicate some meaning if they are read alone, even without musical background. The activity will work best if the vocabulary in the song is fairly common, if there are ample repetitions, and if the enunciation of the singers is fairly clear. Play the song or songs to yourself and try to listen to the words: can you hear the words clearly?

In class

1. Announce the title of the song and the names of the song writer and singer. Tell the students the purpose of the activity — to think about how lyrics and music together create a meaning for the song. Read the lyrics of the song aloud. Ask the students to write down a few words to express 'images' in the song.

2. Now play the recording of the song. Again ask the students to write down any new or changed images they have after hearing the lyrics put to music.

Variation 21.1: Listen for this!

Write down several key phrases from a song, in their chronological order in the song. Play the recording of the song. Ask the students to identify the phrases as they hear them. Many students will learn to hear the words in songs quickly (even if there are some gaps in their knowledge) if they have several 'stable phrases' given to them in writing.

Variation 21.2: Elicit the words

On the blackboard, write out blank lines for the song lyrics, with relative length showing the length of each word. (You may also wish to give the first letter of each word as additional help.) Play the song several times. After each playing, ask for volunteers to fill in whatever words they can. Provide some assistance if the students cannot identify all of the words after four or five hearings.

— ⎯⎯ ⎯⎯⎯ ⎯⎯⎯ ⎯⎯⎯ ⎯⎯⎯⎯⎯

⎯⎯⎯⎯ ⎯⎯⎯⎯⎯⎯ ⎯⎯⎯⎯⎯⎯ ⎯⎯⎯⎯ ⎯⎯⎯⎯

Follow-up options

1. Distribute transcripts of the song. Ask the students to underline expressions (words or phrases) that create strong images. Read through the lyrics again. Then ask the students if their expressions were stressed (received phonological prominence — greater length or loudness than the surrounding words or phrases).

2. Ask students what differences they experience in understanding a song by listening to its lyrics alone, by hearing the lyrics in song, and by listening to the lyrics *and* reading them together.

3. Ask the students to bring in songs whose English lyrics have impressed them in some way.

4. Ask the students to prepare short presentations on the music of their countries. What are some of the traditional songs? children's songs? currently popular songs? Ask the students to provide English translations of the lyrics.

Links

Consider trying activities 3, 9 and 31 as a follow-up to this activity.

Teacher's diary

Did your students enjoy this kind of activity? Do they find it useful for language learning? What other uses of songs do you know?

---

22 Recorded messages

Level	Intermediate and advanced
Students	Young adults and adults
Purpose	Develop strategy of listening for selected information
Text type	Audio tape; announcements

In this activity ...

Students listen to messages (real or simulated announcements and other recorded information) and note down key words and phrases. This activity provides exposure to different types of authentic discourse.

Preparation

1. Collect several authentic recorded messages, such as actual recordings from telephone answering machines or recorded information from public and private services (museum exhibits, cinema schedules, bus timetables, event announcements, school closings) or make your own simulated recordings.

2. For each recorded message, prepare a simple grid or gapped sentence which focuses upon the key information (see the bus schedule example opposite).

Sample tape segment

Thank you for calling Southwest Transit Systems. This is a recorded message to give you the schedule and fares for buses from Los Angeles to our major destinations — San Francisco, Phoenix, and Salt Lake City. If you have questions about other routes, please dial area code 213–711–1177.

Buses for San Francisco leave from Los Angeles Terminal every hour on the half hour, from 5:30 a.m. to 11:30 p.m. Duration of the trip is approximately 8 hours. The one-way fare is $27.50.

Buses for Phoenix depart at 6:20 a.m., 9:20 a.m., 1:20 p.m. and 5:40 p.m.

Southwest Transit Systems			
Bus Schedule			
from Los Angeles to:			
	Departure times I	Arrival times I	Fare (one way/round trip)
San Francisco			
Phoenix			
Salt Lake City			

In class

1. Distribute the information sheets. Go over the information required by the grid. Ask the students to use situation clues to make predictions of the information. For example: which will cost more — the fare to San Francisco or to Phoenix? (Consult a US map for a likely answer.) About how much do you think the fare is to San Francisco? (Consult a map and compare with similar distances in your own area.) How often do you think departures might be between major cities? (Use local comparisons: how often are bus departures between major cities near you?)

2. *Just before* playing the tape, give each student a different destination, and have that student fill in only the information that is relevant to him or her.

Variation 22.1: Service encounters

Use recorded conversations (preferably recorded in the actual situation) of someone obtaining information in a 'service encounter'. ('Service encounters' are live interactions with a 'professional', usually related to obtaining information, goods, or services.) Possible sources are: hotel clerk and guest, bank clerk and customer, shop assistant and customer. Prepare information grids that the students fill out as they listen.

Follow-up options

1. Correction: the students can work in pairs (with someone who had the same

'listening purpose') to compare the information they have in their grids. Play the tape once again to confirm correct answers.

2. Suggest some topics that students can 'research' locally by consulting information services. Schedules of upcoming concerts, lectures, events? Current exhibits at museums and galleries? Train schedules to . . . ? Best local price of a certain model of (computer)? Pose two or three specific questions for each student (or student team). Ask the students to gather the information before the next class.

Links

Consider trying activities 7, 11 and 30.1 as a follow-up to this activity.

Teacher's diary

Do you think using 'authentic recordings' is effective for building listening skills? Do you think that the amount of preparation you had to do for this activity is excessive? Can you keep a file of material for future use (and save time in the future)?

---

23   Facts and figures

Level	Elementary and above, depending on input
Students	Young adults and adults
Purpose	Develop strategy of listening for specific information
Text type	Audio tape or teacher's prepared talk

In this activity ...

Students listen to factual descriptions of people, places, and things. They record the key information on grids.

Preparation

1. Locate a source book of useful information and find topics of interest and value to your students. Almanacs or books of records, such as *The Guinness Book of Records*, are useful for 'light' lessons on a range of topics. Frequently, monthly magazines and special interest periodicals provide interesting compilations of facts and factual accounts on topics of international importance.

2. Record on audio tape a short account that incorporates a set of facts. You can embellish your account with extra detail, but the students in the initial part of the exercise will be asked to focus mainly on the facts and figures.

3. Prepare a 'fact sheet', which has a grid of questions (or cue words) which can be answered while listening to the tape (see the example on the next page). You may wish to prepare multiple-choice items, rather than open-ended questions, initially.

In class

1. Distribute the fact sheets. Ask the students to give their own answers to the questions first, working individually or in pairs. Allow the students time to read through these questions by themselves, or read them aloud as the students read to themselves.

Fastest growing plant	
Most poisonous plant	
Requires the most water	
Grows to the greatest height	
Is most common	
Has the greatest number of species	

2. Play the tape. Students should write down the correct answer, and indicate whether their answer was right. If you play this as a game, ask for a tally: how many people got them all right?

Sample tape segment

Look at the list of items on your fact sheet. Please answer the questions first yourself as the questions are read to you. Then listen to the correct answers.

(1) What is the fastest growing plant? is it the pineapple plant? is it bamboo? or is it an oak tree? Write down your answer.
(2) Which of the following plants is most poisonous? . . .

Variation 23.1: Documentary

Find an authentic source, such as a documentary programme, which has a number of facts presented. News programmes, historical, biographical, and environmental documentaries and science specials are all possible sources. Prepare a fact sheet, in a chronological order corresponding to the commentary of the programme, and distribute this sheet to the students. Have the students provide their own answers (or guesses) *before* listening, so that they will be actively predicting and verifying as they listen to the programme. (After preparing your fact sheet, be sure to try to fill it in as you listen, to make sure that the task is realistic.)

Follow-up options

1. If you have a book of facts or world records, allow some students to page through

it and jot down topic areas that are of interest to them. From their notes, you can make the audio tapes or script notes for the next round of this activity.

2. Ask the students to assemble lists of facts under different headings (e.g. science, geography, sports) and arrange a simple 'true or false' game show.

Links

Consider trying activities 4.2, 12.2 and 32 as a follow-up to this activity.

Teacher's diary

How did your students do in this activity? Do you have suggestions for making the activity more interesting or challenging or more 'authentic'? What other topics would be possible for this activity?

---

24 Story maps

Level   Advanced

Students   Adults

Purpose   Develop organisation skill; develop recall ability

Text type   Audio tape, video tape, or text read aloud; stories

In this activity ...

Students hear a narrative and construct a 'map' of the story, giving the initial characters, setting, problem, course of action to solve the problem, solution, and consequences.

Preparation

1. Find a story (or recall one from your own experience) with an interesting theme, preferably a story that has a 'problem-solution' structure. Political and business dramas are possible sources, as well as folk tales and children's stories. Construct a simplified account of the story, highlighting the main ideas and eliminating distracting detail. Be sure to make explicit the initial characters, the setting, the problem, the course of action, and the outcome.

> NOTE: *Even for young adults and adults, children's stories, which are designed for first language learners, can provide stimulating and effective listening practice. Obtain original cassettes from the many publishers of fine audio materials. A few sources are: Caedmon Listening Library, Random House School Division, Scholastic/ Reader's Choice, Spoken Arts, Simon & Schuster Speaking Books, etc.*

2. Prepare a grid — the story 'map' — in which the students will write notes in appropriate parts to complete the story.

    Sample story map (reduced size)

                               ●
    Characters: ●
                               ●

Setting: *place:*
                 time:

The problem:

The goal:

Actions taken to reach the goal:
-
-
-

Outcome:

In class

1. Distribute the story maps. Explain the purpose of the activity — to listen to the story in order to find out its basic organisation or plan.

2. Play the tape of the story — or narrate the story — one time. Allow the students time to try to complete the story map with as much of the information as they can. (The students can work in pairs or groups to do this.)

3. Provide some hints about any parts of the story map that the students cannot fill in.

4. Play or narrate the story a final time. Discuss different variations of the completed story map.

Variation 24.1: Predict the next part

Narrate the story, but stop when a new event is about to happen or a decision is about to be made. Ask the students for predictions about what will happen next. (Many children's stories are excellent for this purpose.) Be sure to encourage any plausible continuation, and not wait for the only 'correct' one.

Variation 24.2: Argument map

Provide an excerpt from a political speech or editorial in which the speaker is making a strong claim (for example, 'X will be the most urgent medical crisis of the next century' or 'If Y is elected president, our country's economy will be destroyed'). What kind of information is being used to back up this claim? What kind of accepted principles or morals are being used to support the claim? After listening to the speech or editorial, have your students try to make an 'argument map' which clearly shows the claim, the backing (facts which back up the claim), and the principles (ideas or morals which support the claim). This kind of exercise can be useful for drawing attention to the 'rhetoric' of persuasive speeches.

Follow-up options

1. Ask the students to outline and then narrate alternative versions of the story. Ask them to identify on the 'story map' what has changed in the basic organisation.

2. Ask the students to write out (true or fictional) stories that have a problem-solution pattern. Collect the stories and use the best ones for subsequent listening practice.

3. Ask the students to collect folk tales from their own country. Prepare English versions that will be usable for 'story mapping'.

4. Try out this activity with video. Choose dramatic segments from situation comedies, 'soap opera' dramas, or full-length Hollywood films.

Links

Consider trying activities 4, 29 and 35 as a follow-up to this activity.

Teacher's diary

Did the mapping activity increase your students' interest in the stories? Did it help them to understand or recall the stories? Can you think of ways to explore how to understand 'typical' stories with your students? Are there any significant cultural issues involved in understanding stories?

---

25   Talk show

Level   Advanced

Students   Adults

Purpose   Develop ability to listen for gist, develop note-taking skills

Text type   Audio tape or video tape; broadcast

In this activity ...

Students listen to a segment of a talk show. They identify topics that are introduced and one main point made by each speaker.

Preparation

1. Find an interesting segment of a talk show or interview show on video tape or audio tape. Sources may be regularly televised shows, especially those featuring controversial topics with panelists giving their views.

2. Listen to the segment yourself. Note down any areas of vocabulary that you think may present difficulties for your students.

3. Make a simple visual sketch to show the speakers involved in the talk show. Under each speaker's image write the words: TOPICS, STATEMENTS, VIEWS. A visual representation is easier if using video; some means of identifying speakers on audio tape should be devised.

In class

1. Distribute the visual sketches. Tell the students that they are to fill in as much as they can about each of the speakers after watching the talk show segment.

2. Preview some of the key vocabulary. Give example sentences in contexts similar to those in the show, but without providing key information from the show.

3. Play one segment of the talk show or interview. Ask the students to fill in: What *topics* did they discuss? What *statements* (paraphrases, not exact words) did each speaker make? What *views* (opinions) did each speaker give?

4. Let students watch or listen to the full sequence, unsegmented.

Variation 25.1: Whose line?

List several of the phrases used by the speakers on the tape on the blackboard. Read over the lines with the class. Play the taped segment. At the end of the segment, students categorise the phrases by speaker: Who said each line? This simple exercise can help students sort out and remember what they have heard and understood.

Variation 25.2: Opinion gap

Prepare your own interview tape, or monologue tape (that is, a sequence of monologues by different speakers), in which two speakers give complementary or somewhat opposing views on a topic. The topic might be a moral or social dilemma in which two speakers give their proposed solutions. Or the topic might be a social issue which invites a range of overlapping viewpoints. After the students have listened to each extract once or twice, ask them first to note the main points of each argument. The students can then discuss: are the arguments opposed? are they complementary? which argument is stronger or more compelling?

Follow-up options

1. Ask the students to prepare and produce their own talk show. Guests (other students or 'outsiders') should be selected on the basis of prior written responses to a set of questions. Select speakers who have particularly coherent viewpoints.

2. Present part of a transcript of the show. Highlight some of the appropriate discourse cues used by the speakers in the conversation. Which of them show that they are actively listening (cues such as 'um-hmm' or 'oh, really')? Also point out some of the 'agreement markers' that the speakers use (cues such as 'I see what you mean', 'good point', 'right', 'I agree with you up to a point, but . . .').

3. Discuss with your students the normal difficulties of understanding native speakers in authentic conversations with each other. Note that there are important factors that make authentic conversations understandable to the participants, but not to an outside listener — shared background knowledge (similar past experiences and type of education) and shared topics (things they talked about earlier). Not all of the difficulties they experience are directly related to their language ability! Encourage the students to be satisfied with understanding the main points and the speakers' attitudes in overheard conversations.

Links

Consider trying activities 8, 12.1, 15, 29.1 and 37.1 as a follow-up to this activity.

Teacher's diary

What video resources, including local television, do you have that may be useful for this activity? What are some other ways you have discovered to involve students in the viewing of authentic interviews and programmes?

26　In order

Level　　　　　Intermediate and advanced

Students　　　Young adults and adults

Purpose　　　Develop ability to listen for discourse markers; develop aural memory

Text type　　Audio tape; conversation

In this activity ...

Students listen to dialogues. The students are given strips of paper with single lines of the dialogue written on them. The students put the lines in order.

Preparation

1.　Locate several recorded conversations on the same topic, or in the same setting and situation (e.g. at a hotel, guest checking in). There should be enough turns to make this activity challenging — about twelve turns for each conversation. Make a transcript of the conversation and cut it into strips, with one speaker turn per strip. (Sound effects, if any, should also be noted on the strips.)

2.　Play the tape recording of the conversations to yourself and attempt to put the strips in order as you listen. If this is too difficult to do (perhaps because the turns are too short), combine two turns per strip.

3.　Copy enough strips for all your students.

In class

1.　Distribute the strips to the students in jumbled order. Tell them the setting of the conversation. Can they put the strips in order, even without hearing the conversation? Give them a few minutes to try to do this.

2.　Play the tape once. Ask the students to listen only without manipulating the strips. After the first playing, allow another minute for the students to arrange their strips in order according to the tape.

3.   Play the tape a second time for confirmation.

Variation 26.1: Monologues

This activity can be done with sets of instructions (e.g. recipes), or with narratives, or with news broadcasts. Prepare a transcript and cut it into parts that correspond to 'event chunks' in the story or to segments of the broadcast. Ask the students to memorise their strips. In order to put the script together, the students will listen to you read the entire script aloud once. Then (in groups) they recite their own bits, listen to each other, and pay attention to different sequence cues.

Follow-up options

1.   For each conversation, discuss with the class how they were able to put the conversation in order. What are the sequence cues? Were some of the exchanges 'routines' that are very predictable? Did some of the turns have pronoun references (*one*, *that*, *it*, *them*) that showed a connection to other turns?

2.   Compare the different conversations in the same setting and situation. How are they alike — do they have common patterns? How are they different — are there different ways to reach the same conversational goal?

Links

Consider trying activities 7.1, 11.1, 14.1, 25.1 and 36.1 as a follow-up to this activity.

Teacher's diary

How did your students do in this activity? What are the advantages of having the students do this activity alone? In small groups? Do you think that this kind of study of 'cohesion clues' will help develop your students' listening ability?

27 Topic listening

Level	Intermediate and advanced
Students	Young adults and adults
Purpose	Develop ability to listen for main ideas; develop note-taking and review skills
Text type	Teacher's prepared presentation; lectures

In this activity ...

Students study a topic area (academic or technical) through short lectures, which are supported by readings and in-class discussions and presentations.

Preparation

1. Select a subject area on which you can give a series of short informal lectures. This might be an academic area such as political history (e.g. a biography of a significant person), biology (e.g. an account of a particular discovery), or philosophy (e.g. a review of thinking at a particular period of history). It might be a non-academic area such as local history, parapsychology, or tournament billiards. The topic should be of interest to you and your students, and it should be a topic that you know fairly well. You should also have ample resource material (including visuals) in order to prepare a few informative lectures and presentations.

2. Prepare notes for two or three short lectures. Also prepare a true/false test for each lecture. The true/false tests should cover the main content of the lecture and ask for both factual recall and inference.

In class

1. Distribute the true/false test *in advance of the lecture*. Read over the items with the students. To how many do they know the answer already, *before* the lecture even starts? (They should not be able to answer more than half the questions without listening to the lecture, or else the lecture content and test are too easy.) Collect

the blank tests and tell the students you will distribute them again at the end of the lecture.

2. Deliver your lecture informally, allowing questions as you go along. If possible, tape-record the lecture for later reference. Encourage the students to take notes, particularly about items they remember to be on the upcoming test.

3. When you have finished the lecture, distribute the true/false tests again. After the students have taken the test, go over the answers with them.

Variation 27.1: Write your questions

If students do not seem to be following the lecture *and* are reticent about asking you clarification questions, stop the lecture periodically and ask *every student* to write down one question about the lecture on a slip of paper. Collect the slips quickly and read out some of the questions and respond to them, without giving the identity of the questioner. Eventually, as the students become more confident about asking questions, you should be able to drop the step of actually having the students write out their questions.

Variation 27.2: Standard questions

By having students compare their own test questions with those written by test experts, the students can become more aware of inferential types of question that are often used in standardised tests. Have your students take a practice test for a standardised test, such as the Test of English as a Foreign Language (TOEFL). Allow the students to hear each lecture segment in advance, before they see the prepared test questions. Ask the students to prepare their own questions. Then let them compare their questions with those written by the test writer. Which are similar?

Follow-up options

1. Ask the students to reconstruct lecture notes into short oral (or written) summaries.

2. Ask the students to do short research projects related to the lecture topic. These can be the basis for oral presentations to the class.

Links

Consider trying activities 4.2, 12.2 and 32 as a follow-up to this activity.

Teacher's diary

How did your students do in this activity? Were there any special problems in preparing the activity? How did you deal with vocabulary that might be unfamiliar to the students? What kind of help did the students need to follow the lecture? Do you have suggestions for improving the lecture next time?

28 Conversation clues

Level	Intermediate and advanced
Students	Adults
Purpose	Develop skill in making inferences based on known information; develop test-taking skill
Text type	Audio tape; conversations

In this activity ...

Students listen to short conversations and make guesses about each conversation: setting, relationships between the people, the purpose.

Preparation

1. Obtain tape recordings of several short conversations which are not necessarily related to each other. (One possible resource is practice tests in TOEFL (Test of English as a Foreign Language) test preparation books, which sometimes contain random sequences of conversations followed by recall questions and inference questions.)

2. Listen to the recordings and write down two or three questions for each that are answerable from the conversation. (1) *Setting:* what is the setting? where does this conversation probably take place? (2) *Characters:* who are the speakers? what is the relationship between the speakers? (3) *Purpose:* what is the purpose of the conversation? what does A want B to do? why did A say (...)? (4) *Attitude of the speakers:* what is A's attitude towards B? what is A's reaction to B?

In class

1. As a warm-up activity, write the names of several occupations on the chalkboard: doctor, dentist, teacher, mechanic, sales clerk, postal clerk, hairdresser, police officer. Ask the students what words and phrases they think each person often uses. For instance, if you say 'teacher', the students may suggest words such as 'books' and 'homework', and phrases such as 'OK, let's continue' or 'today,

I'd like to . . .'. Write the words and phrases on the board. Continue with some of the other occupations.

2. Explain the purpose of the upcoming listening activity — to listen *without* knowing the context and to find clues to the setting by using background knowledge.

3. Play each conversation. At the end of the conversation, ask your questions. The students write down brief answers.

4. After playing the sequence of conversations, go back to the first one and replay it. Ask the questions again and elicit answers from the students. Ask them what clues in the conversation helped them to answer the questions. Specific words and expressions? Intonation? Repetition? Predictable patterns in the conversations?

Variation 28.1: Which was it?

Play the short conversations again. For each conversation, write out one of the lines in two or three different versions. Each version of the line should have the same basic meaning (although the social register or social effect may be somewhat different). For example, if the line is: *'can you tell me where the bus stop is?'* use paraphrases such as:

- *Do you know where the bus stop is?*
- *Would you happen to know where the bus stop is?*
- *Please tell me where the bus stop is.*

After listening to the conversation, the students select the *exact* line that the speaker said. Play the tape a final time so that students can verify the exact form of the utterance.

Variation 28.2: Test questions

Prepare, or locate, several two-line dialogues which require a 'fill-in link' to be understood. An example:

> MAN: *The front tyre is flat and the shock absorbers need to be replaced.*
> WOMAN: *Better take it to Mr Jones.*

Students, working in pairs, will be given the transcript for one conversation. They are to write a 'test question' on the dialogue, which cannot be answered *directly* from information in the dialogue. For example:

> Question: *What kind of work does Mr Jones probably do?*

By attempting this kind of question writing, the students should become better able to anticipate test questions.

Follow-up options

1. Ask the students to write several short conversations which have one or two cues about the relationship between the speakers or the setting. Possibilities for settings are: customs and immigration at an airport, bank transactions, post office, department store, restaurants and cafés, travel agencies, train stations. Pairs of students say their conversations (without miming any actions). Can others guess the relationship and the setting?

2. Let the students take a practice listening test of any standardised test which has short taped conservations and written multiple choice answers to questions. Go over the test results as a class to analyse *how* the correct answers were found.

Links

Consider trying activities 11, 13, 34.1 and 37 as a follow-up to this activity.

Teacher's diary

Were the students successful in using context clues to help them in the activity? Do the students like to have 'test questions' following each conversation? If so, why? If not, why not?

---

29 Episode

Level   Intermediate and advanced

Students   Adults

Purpose   Develop ability to listen for gist; develop skill of identifying missing information prior to listening

Text type   Video tape; broadcast

In this activity ...

Students listen to an episode from a TV drama or from a video tape of a feature-length film. They complete a basic comprehension check quiz and a review form.

Preparation

1. Select an interesting five- to ten-minute segment from a television drama, film, or English Language Teaching (ELT) serial drama. Alternatively, you may select audio-only sources, including 'read-along novels'.

2. Watch (or listen to) the drama yourself. Prepare a 'gapped' paragraph which constitutes a general summary of each segment. Leave out key actions (verb phrases) and key descriptions (adjective phrases), rather than names and details of time and place.

    Sample gapped paragraph

    (Based on a detective story)

    This is the story of a man named Arthur Logo who died on the evening of December 31st. Police Lieutenant Walala contacted Martha Lowes, who said that she and Logo went to a party together that evening. Ms Lowes denied any involvement in the murder, but police said that ...

    (The underlined portions are to be left blank on the students' sheets.)

3. If you are using an audio-only source, prepare some simple visual aids which will help contextualise the segment.

In class

1. Introduce the new segment of the story by recounting, or asking one of the students to recount, the previous episode.

2. Pose two or three 'inferential' questions that will be answered in the upcoming episode. (For example, why couldn't Ms Lowes have been with him on that night? What did she mean when she said she knew Mr Logo 'only professionally'?)

3. Play the episode in its entirety, without stopping. Ask the students which of your advance questions they can or cannot respond to. Don't provide answers to the questions yourself at this point, but do suggest where in the episode some relevant information to the question can be located.

4. Elicit further questions from the students, again directing them to places in the tape to listen for answers. Play the segment again.

5. Distribute the gapped paragraph and provide time for the students to complete the summary. You may wish to have them work in pairs on the summary. Allow approximate answers for the fill-ins.

Follow-up options

1. The students re-enact the scene in their own words. Attention should focus on the meaning of the scene and the attitudes of the characters, not on the exact wording.

2. Discuss the scene with the students. Are there any interesting cultural insights to be gained from the scene?

3. Discuss with the students how to set up a self-access centre so that they can listen regularly to tapes of the kind used in this activity. (See following variation 29.1: Self-access.)

Variation 29.1: Self-access

Provide a facility for self-access listening or viewing and a realistic time when students can use the facility. Prepare several short audio and video tape programmes for students at different levels (beginning, intermediate, advanced). Try to vary the selection of recorded materials: serial mysteries, music videos, short stories, folk tales and fables (including children's stories), non-fiction documentaries, social conversations, simulated lectures. Prepare a reporting sheet (see sample on the next page) for the students to use with each programme.

The initial investment of time, energy, and money in setting up a **self-access listening programme** for your students will be significant but the long-term benefits will make it worth the effort. One of the essential features of any successful self-access centre is *teacher* follow-up: regular checking of learners' journals, keeping records of time each student spends in the self-access centre, chatting with learners regularly about the content of the programmes they listen to.

In the initial stages of organising a self-access programme, it may be useful to assemble a set of original copies of audio and video tapes that are likely to be of interest to the students. Develop a simple indexing system for the tapes you have available. Ask the students to read through the list of tape titles (with brief descriptions of the contents and length of the tape) and to rate each title in terms of interest on a 0-1-2-3 scale.

Self-access report sample (reduced size: the actual form should have enough space for writing)

BEFORE LISTENING:
1. *What tape are you going to listen to or watch?*
2. *Why did you choose this tape?*
3. *How long are you planning to listen today?*
4. *What do you expect to learn from this tape?*
5. *How will you listen to the tape?*
    (a) Listen to the whole tape and try to understand the overall meaning.
    (b) Listen and replay sections that I don't understand well.

WHILE YOU LISTEN:
Write notes on the main events and ideas of the tape.

AFTER YOU LISTEN:
Write a 25-word summary of the tape: list 10 expressions from the tape that you would like to be able to use.

OPINION:
1. *Do you recommend this tape to other students? Why or why not?*
2. *Please prepare a short (5-minute) quiz on this tape. Also provide an answer key.*

Links

Consider trying activity 36.2 as a follow-up to this activity.

Teacher's diary

What aspects of the drama were most interesting to the students?
Did any of the students have particular cultural insights to share
after listening to or viewing the episode? In the follow-up
re-enactment, did the students recreate the 'meaning' of the
scene effectively?

SECTION IV

INTERACTIVE LISTENING

Introduction

One of the true tests of listening ability in a second language is participating in social interaction in very small groups. Especially in pair interactions, the listeners must continuously identify new information, work out problems they encounter trying to understand each other, and formulate responses in 'real time' in order to keep the interaction going. One way to prepare our learners for this real-world test is to involve them in classroom activities in which the *learners work together* on interactive problem-solving tasks. In addition to the important social benefits of this kind of activity, learning to work out language problems is important for second-language development.

In order to highlight the interaction between listening and speaking in language development, the activities in this section involve both comprehension and production. In particular, the activities involve the following steps:

1. Setting up learning activities in which the students, not the teacher, play the central role.

2. Setting forth specific goals so that the students can assess their own work.

3. Focusing on teacher observation of the students' language during the activities in order to provide feedback on their interaction strategies.

The **key features** of the activities in this section are:

- The learners work in pairs and small groups.
- The learners work on problem-solving tasks.
- The learners receive immediate feedback through their success in the task.

- The teacher directs a review of language used during the activity.
- The teacher prepares visual and written materials in advance.

There are eight basic activity outlines in this section. As in other sections, the activities have variations with similar instructional goals.

30. Group survey
   Variation 30.1: Project journalist

31. Self-introductions
   Variation 31.1: Biography

32. Short speeches
   Variation 32.1: Impromptu speeches

Variation 32.2: Future plans

33. **Map route**
Variation 33.1: Diagrams
Variation 33.2: Cartoon squares
Variation 33.3: Blindfolds

34. **Picture differences**
Variation 34.1: Cartoon sequences
Variation 34.2: Angles

35. **Recounted stories**
Variation 35.1: Complete the story

36. **Testimony**
Variation 36.1: Fill the gap
Variation 36.2: Assemble the script

37. **Conversation tips**
Variation 37.1: Listener diary

There are a number of 'real-world links' to the interactive listening activities in this section:

• chatting and discussing topics with friends
• making arrangements
• exchanging news, reports, or anecdotes
• interviewing and being interviewed
• working collaboratively on projects

The activities in this section can be used with learners at various levels, from beginning to advanced. As with activities in other sections of *Listening in Action*, particular activities can be adjusted for your learner groups. Beginning students will find information-gap activities such as *Map route* and *Picture differences* (as well as the variations provided) useful for language practice, provided that the teacher selects appropriate 'input materials' and provides clear, supportive steps for the in-class procedures. Intermediate learners will benefit from activities such as *Group survey, Self-introductions*, and *Short speeches*, all of which allow for interactive practice with new language forms that the learners may be practising. Advanced learners will find the open-ended activities such as *Testimony* and *Recounted stories* stimulating and challenging in that the activities call for personal interpretation and imagination.

In general, all your students should find the activities in this section enjoyable and challenging since they involve both listening and speaking (as well as reading and writing in many of the follow-up steps). Experiment with the 'preparation' procedures in order to make the activities as authentic (similar to situations of real language use) as possible. For instance, in *Map route*, ask the students to bring in maps of the school and community in order to practise immediately useful vocabulary items. Similarly, for *Short speeches*, ask the students regularly to prepare presentations on current events and topics of local interest.

In order to increase the learning value of these interaction activities, also consider exploiting the follow-up procedures. Many of the follow-ups draw the students' attention to *how* they used language during the activity, thus increasing opportunities for observing and developing their own grammar and usage. Most of the follow-ups also provide extension links to out-of-class language use.

30 Group survey

Level	Elementary and above, depending on input
Students	Young adults and adults
Purpose	Develop ability to initiate interactions; encourage careful listening to classmates
Text type	Prepared questions; survey

In this activity ...

Students work in small groups to complete personal surveys. They then report back to the whole class.

Preparation

1. Select an appropriate topic area that will stimulate conversation among your students:

    *   favourite foods, clothes, or music
    *   opinions about recent films
    *   leisure time activities
    *   childhood recollections
    *   future plans
    *   attitudes about a particular environmental, social, or political issue
    *   reactions to a hypothetical situation (*what would you do if* ...)
    *   imaginary scenarios (*what would people be able to do if they had seven fingers and two thumbs? what would we do differently if our human life expectancy were 180 years?*)

2. Identify the grammatical forms that will be needed by your students in answering the questionnaire.

3. Write an interesting questionnaire of eight to ten items that your students will answer. Provide a range of question types.

In class

1. Ask the students to work in groups of three or four. Distribute the questionnaires. Ask the group to look through the questionnaire and decide on five questions (of the ten given) they would like to ask one another.

2. List on the board the main grammatical forms that the students can refer to as they ask and answer the survey questions.

3. Give the students ample time to ask one another the questions. Each person should note the others' answers, though there is no need to write down the answers verbatim. Encourage elaboration in the answers to the questions.

4. At the end, compile the results of the questionnaires. Ask each group: which answers seemed most original? most insightful? which brought most agreement? most disagreement?

Variation 30.1: Project journalist

Help the students arrange projects which call for out-of-class interviews. These might be interviews with teachers, other students, local residents, tourists, etc. Work carefully with the students in planning what kind of information they will need to gather, whom they will interview, where, and when. If the project involves interviewing strangers, practise in class some basic 'politeness routines' for interviewing strangers. (For example, 'Excuse me, I'm from The ABC Language Institute and we're doing a survey about eating habits. Can I ask you a few questions?') Ask the students to bring the results of the interviews to the class and discuss what they found out.

Follow-up options

1. Each group chooses one question which seemed the most interesting. It creates two or three additional questions and gives this questionnaire to one of the other groups, or other classes in the school.

2. Provide a short grammar lesson. If you noted any *consistent* difficulties with the targeted grammar forms, a short explanation of the grammar points may help. You might then prepare a similar survey exercise for the next class, using different content but the same grammar target, so that students can practise using the form contrast again.

3. Prepare a tape of native speakers or fluent non-native speakers using the same questionnaire with each other. Play this tape to the class in order to give the students a comparative version.

Links

Consider trying activities 4.1, 13 and 25 as a follow-up to this activity.

Teacher's diary

How well did the activity go? Which topics and questions generated the most discussion? Can you think of some ideas for class projects that would involve the students in interviewing others in English?

---

31 Self-introductions

Level	All levels
Students	Young adults
Purpose	Develop ability to listen for gist; develop ability to ask information and clarification questions
Text type	Student presentations

In this activity ...

Students prepare short self-introductions. All students listen to the self-introductions in class and make brief notes about each of their classmates.

Preparation

1. Each student in the class prepares a short (about one minute) self-introduction. Write out the following questions (or variations of them) and give them to the students before they prepare their self-introduction:

    *   *Tell us about your background (where are you from? who are the members of your family?).*
    *   *Tell us about your interests (what do you like to do in your free time?).*
    *   *Tell us about your future goals (what plans do you have for the future?).*
    *   *Tell us one thing you do better than most people.*

    The self-introductions can be performed 'live' or 'on tape'. If they are to be done on tape, they should be done partially (not completely) scripted by the students. Have the introduction recorded in a separate room or studio on audio or video tape, in after-class hours. One alternative to monologue self-introductions is for the teacher to hold short interviews with each student. These interviews can be recorded on audio or video tape.

2. Prepare a simple grid listing each student's name, with a small square for each category: *background, interests, future plans, what he or she does better than most people.*

Variation 31.1: Biography

Each student takes the role of a famous person — a movie star, a historical figure, etc. Give the students time to 'research' their character. (Real facts about the character are usually preferable to fantasy in this activity.) Conduct the self-introductions in the same way.

In class

1. The students give their self-introductions, either live or via an audio or video tape. Students listen to the introduction and write a word or phrase for each box in their grid.

2. At the end of each introduction, the teacher and the other students ask elaboration questions of the student who was just introduced.

Follow-up options

1. The students attempt to remember one thing about each classmate. One student begins by introducing himself or herself and saying one thing he or she has done (for example, 'I'm Max. I like to swim in my free time'). The next student continues by repeating the information and adding his own ('Max likes to swim in his free time. I'm Lea. I like to read novels in my free time'). The third student repeats the information about the first two and adds on. The round continues until all students have added information. (You might want to have the students go in a random order — and have some of the earlier students repeat their lines — in order that all the students' attention is on remembering the information.)

2. Ask the students to interview one or two others in more depth. They should prepare two or three additional questions in advance.

> NOTE: *This basic activity can be done from time to time, each time with new categories (such as opinions about current topics) added.*

3. Ask each student to write a short paragraph about one or two other students in the class. These short paragraphs, along with photographs, can be posted in the classroom.

Links

Consider trying activities 5.1, 6, 18 and 25.2 as a follow-up to this activity.

Teacher's diary

How did the students respond to the self-introductions? What are some other ways for your students to get to know one another better?

32 Short speeches

Level	Intermediate and advanced
Students	Young adults and adults
Purpose	Encourage the asking of clarification and confirmation questions; develop skill of identifying missing information
Text type	Student presentations

In this activity . . .

Students listen to one another give short prepared speeches to the class. Students who are listeners have a simple outline or task sheet to complete as they listen. Following the lecture, the students each ask the speaker one question. Then they fill out a rating form about each speech.

Preparation

1. Prepare the rating forms (see the example opposite, but allow more space for writing). The rating forms should concentrate on general impressions of the speech and the overall effect. Content questions should be rather general: was the explanation clear? complete? convincing? Questions about style might include: did the speaker address the audience respectfully? appropriately? did the speaker's gestures help us to understand the speech?

2. Have all the students submit an outline of their talk to you in advance. Prepare a basic outline of each student's talk for the listener students to fill in while the speaker is giving his or her speech.

3. Students should be given guidelines for preparing and delivering their speeches well in advance of the day speeches are given to the class. If possible, provide the students with opportunities to practise their speeches in very small groups first.

In class

1. Encourage the speakers to work from notes only, not to read their speeches. Allow each speaker the same amount of time.

Name of speaker _____

Topic _____   Length of speech _____

This speech was (place a tick in one of the boxes)

☐   ☐   ☐

---

well organised   not well organised

The speaker's topic was

☐   ☐   ☐

---

very interesting   not so interesting

• One thing that I learned from this speech:

• One question I would like to ask the speaker:

---

2. Students will be making brief notes on the speech outlines as they listen. Allow for questions either during the speech itself, or during a brief question—answer period just afterwards.

3. Collect the rating cards at the end of each speech. (If the cards are written anonymously, they may subsequently be given to the speakers as a kind of feedback on their performance.)

Variation 32.1: Impromptu speeches

Prepare several cards (or ask the students to prepare the cards) on which two general topics are written (e.g. *Pets* or *Health food/Prices today* or *The school system in my country*). Students work in groups. Each student selects a card and has a minute to choose one of the topics and prepare a one-minute impromptu speech. The other students in the group fill out a similar 'feedback form'. By working in small groups, the students will usually be less nervous and will gain more direct practice time.

Variation 32.2: Future plans

Working in pairs, one student begins to tell a story about his or her weekend plans (or plans for the summer holidays, etc.). The story can be real or make-believe. After each sentence, the partner asks 'and after that?' The student continues the story. Each time he or she finishes a statement, the partner asks the same question. The speaker's goal is to make as many statements as possible. The listener's goal is to try to remember the entire sequence of plans. When the speaker finishes, the students change roles. (If this is done as a contest, the student who makes the most statements is the winner. However, if the partner can recall the whole set of plans, he or she is the winner!)

Follow-up options

1. Students can work in pairs to interview their partners further about the topic they spoke on. The listener should then write a short essay summarising the partner's topic. The partner should read a draft of this essay and check it for accuracy of facts and plausibility of ideas.

2. If you have tape-recorded the student presentations, allow each student to listen to his or her own presentation.

3. Suggest topics for future speeches for each student or elicit new topics from the students. Aim to have the topics become as specific as possible.

Links

Consider trying activities 2, 12.1 and 27 as a follow-up to this activity.

Teacher's diary

How well did the activity go? Did the students who gave their speeches later perform differently from those who went first? If so, how? Did the students listen to each speech? If not, what prevented them from listening? What are some other ways to encourage students to listen to each other in classroom activities and discussions?

---

33 Map route

Level   All levels

Students   Young adults and adults

Purpose   Encourage students to ask clarification and confirmation
                     questions and respond to questions effectively; encourage
                     students to initiate questioning to obtain necessary
                     information

Text type   Student interaction; visual materials

In this activity ...

This is a one-way information gap task. Learners work in pairs, with one instructing
the other how to arrive at a certain destination on the map.

Preparation

1. Make two photocopies of a map (or draw one) that has a number of details on
   it — street names, shops, landmarks, etc. for city maps; highways and roads,
   mountains, rivers, fields, etc. for rural maps.

2. On individual cards or slips of paper write the names of several destinations. These
   should be places that can be located on the map, but which are not explicitly
   labelled. For example:

   IBM Building, Mr Donut Coffee Shop, Post Office. On other slips of paper, write
   several 'starting points'. During the classroom task, each student pair will choose
   from a set of destinations and starting points.

In class

1. Provide a sample demonstration of the procedure, with a map. You can be the
   speaker and one of the students the listener:

   *TEACHER: I'm going to tell you how to to get to the IBM Building ... What's
   your starting point? (student chooses from the pile of 'starting point'
   cards)*

STUDENT: *It's the First Street Bus Terminal.*

TEACHER: *OK, let's see . . . from the First Street Bus Terminal . . . you have to go up First Street until you get to the Monument Traffic Circle . . . do you see that?*

STUDENT: *Yes.*

TEACHER: *Then turn right . . . that's Monument Boulevard . . . go down Monument Boulevard . . .*

Have the listener trace the route on the map.

2. Point out to the students that as you direct the listener, he or she will most likely *need to ask you questions for clarification* (e.g. Did you say 'right'? 'Can you repeat that?' 'Do you mean . . .?'). Make a mental note of the questions that the student volunteer asks you during the demonstration; after the task is completed, write some of these clarification questions on the board, telling the students that these kinds of questions are *necessary* if they are to do the task successfully.

3. Have the students work in pairs. Distribute the maps and place the destination and starting point cards in a convenient location. Have each pair place a barrier between them (e.g. a pile of books).

4. Ask each pair to find four destinations on the map. Each member of the pair should have two chances to be the direction giver and direction receiver.

Follow-up options

1. Tape-record one or more of the pairs. Use transcripts of parts of the interactions to show the students how clarification questions by the listener can increase efficiency in understanding. (Note that there may also be cases in which *too many* clarification questions confuse the directions!) Also show how occasional use of comprehension checks by the speaker (e.g. 'Do you understand?' 'Have you got that?') can help the interaction go more smoothly.

2. Bring in actual maps of local areas or cities. Ask the students to create map route tasks based on these authentic maps.

Variation 33.1: Diagrams

One student has a finished diagram or block display. This student explains to a partner how to construct or draw the 'target' figure. It may be best to start with very simple diagrams and displays and *gradually* work up to complex ones.

Variation 33.2: Cartoon squares

One student has a cartoon sequence (preferably 6 or 8 squares), with or without dialogue balloons, in proper order. The other student has the same cartoon squares, but out of order. The dialogue balloons, if any, should be separated, so that the 'listener' must also place the correct dialogue with the pictures.

Variation 33.3: Blindfolds

This is an interactive game to promote listening for directions. Place several small markers (coins, chips, or wads of paper) around the room; one student will be given directions to find the markers. One volunteer student is blindfolded (with a scarf). The other students give the blindfolded student directions to the markers. How many markers can the student collect in three minutes?

Links

Consider trying activities 1, 5.2, 10.1 and 20.1 as a follow-up to this activity.

Teacher's diary

How well did the activity go? What are the benefits of having the students working together in pairs and small groups? What are the drawbacks? Did the experience of being in the listener's role sensitise the students to the requirements of the speaker's task? Did you discuss this with the students?

---

34 Picture differences

Level	All levels
Students	All ages
Purpose	Encourage students to listen carefully to partners to obtain specific information; encourage students to initiate questioning to obtain specific information
Text type	Student interaction; visual materials

In this activity ...

Students work in pairs to discover differences between a pair of pictures.

Preparation

1. Select an illustration that has several items in it (e.g. a room with a desk, a person sitting at a desk, a filing cabinet, a door, pictures on the wall). Photocopy the illustration and change several items in one of the copies (e.g. add something to or remove something from the desk, or alter the position of some of the items).

> NOTE: *By selecting the pictures for this activity, you are setting the vocabulary that is needed in the task. This is an effective technique for introducing and practising vocabulary that is needed for specific purposes and 'life skills'.*

2. Make a list of sentences that describe the differences between the pictures.

In class

1. Pair the students. Distribute different pictures to the members of each pair. Tell them there are several differences between the pictures and that they must find the differences *only* by talking to each other.

2. Write these expressions on the blackboard:

Confirm: *Clarify:*
Do you understand?   What do you mean?

Got that?	Did you say . . .?
OK?	I don't understand.
Ask:	*Announce:*
How about in your picture?	Let me start.
Is there a . . . in your picture?	Tell me about the . . .
	OK, that's a difference.
	Good. We found one.

3. Tell the students to circle the differences on their pictures. Allow the students a fixed amount of time. How many differences could each group find?

Variation 34.1: Cartoon sequences

Take a newspaper strip cartoon (4 or 6 frames) and cut it into separate squares. Give half the squares to one student in a pair, half to the other student. Without showing the pictures to each other, the students decide on the sequence of the story.

Variation 34.2: Angles

Make a blank 3-by-3 grid (nine squares). Prepare nine illustrations or photographs that will fit in the squares. After preparing enough copies for your students, cut the illustrations diagonally into halves. Half the students (the 'A' students in each pair) receive one set of 'half pictures', while the other half (the 'B' students in each pair) receive the other 'half pictures'. Each student pair must agree on the position of the nine pictures in their grid. They must exchange information about the pictures to do this. (For example, A: *Let's put the picture of the man with the striped shirt in the top left picture.* B: *Which man?* A: *The man with the striped shirt.* B: *I don't see a man with a striped shirt.* A: *He has a dark sweater.* B: *OK, I see him...*)

Follow-up options

1. Ask which of the differences were hardest to locate. Ask different pairs how they discovered the differences (what did they say to each other?).

2. If you have tape-recorded any of the pairs, play back excerpts from the interaction. Find examples of *effective* negotiation to write on the blackboard as models for future activities of this type.

Links

Consider trying activities 1, 13 and 14.1 as a follow-up to this activity.

Teacher's diary

Did you find any differences in student interaction between the 'one-way information gap' task (*Map route*) and this activity (or any of the variations)? Did the students use their native language during this task? Do you have an agreement with your students about the role of the native language in classroom activities?

35 Recounted stories

Level	Intermediate and advanced
Students	Young adults and adults
Purpose	Increase attention span for listening; develop aural memory
Text type	Students' prepared texts; stories

In this activity ...

Each student retells a story to another student who has not read it. The 'listener' is provided with a list of questioning prompts and is encouraged to ask questions regularly as the story is told. The listener must then reconstruct the story for a third person.

Preparation

1. Locate or make up three short stories, historical accounts, anecdotes, folk tales, riddles, or comic strip sequences that the students will be able to understand without your assistance.

   Sample story (fictional, based on an historical account)

   In the late fall of the year 333 BC the Macedonian general Alexander and his army arrived in the Asian city of Gordium to take up their winter residence there. While in Gordium, Alexander heard about the local legend concerning the city's famous knot, which was called 'The Gordian Knot'. An ancient prophecy stated that the person who was able to untie this strangely complicated knot would become the ruler of all Asia. This legend, and the prophecy, was intriguing to Alexander. Alexander asked the local people to take him to the knot so that he could try his hand at untying it. Upon seeing the complicated knot, Alexander studied it for several minutes. After many fruitless attempts to find the ends of the rope, he became stuck. He asked himself, 'How can I do this?' Suddenly, he came upon an idea: 'I think I'll make up my own rules for untying knots.' So Alexander pulled out his heavy sword and cut the knot in half. Alexander subsequently became the ruler of Asia.

2. Make enough copies of each story for one-third of the class.

In class

1. Have the students work in groups of three. Distribute one different story to each person in the group.

2. For each story, one student is the *story-teller*, one student is the *listener*, and one student is the *auditor*. Explain these roles:
    (a) The story-teller retells his or her story to the listener, without referring back to the written text.
    (b) The listener listens to the story, and asks questions as the story is told, but cannot take notes.
    (c) The auditor writes down the questions that the listener asks.

3. Allow each story-teller one or two minutes prior to telling the story to review the contents. As they tell the story, their copy should not be in sight.

4. During the story telling, listeners should ask questions frequently about information in the story which they do not understand. (For groups whose students share the same native language, encourage the students to use English to ask all their questions.)

5. Auditors should write down all the questions that are asked by the listeners.

Variation 35.1: Complete the story

Use short stories or folk tales. Provide nearly all the story to the listener. The listener must provide one or two plausible endings to the story.

Follow-up options

1. Ask the students to evaluate the activity. What did they learn from the activity? New vocabulary? Ways to tell stories? Ways to ask questions?

2. Ask each student to write out a summary of the story for which he or she was the listener.

3. Group the questions that were noted down by the 'auditors'. Classify these as *questions about general understanding, questions about the meaning of words*, and *questions about facts in the story*. Encourage the students to ask 'questions about facts' as often as they can, rather than to ask only about word meanings (e.g. 'What does . . . mean?') or for general understanding (e.g. 'Can you repeat that?').

4. Ask your students to find (or write) other short texts to bring to the next class.

Links

Consider trying activities 21.1, 24, 26 and 27.1 as a follow-up to this activity.

Teacher's diary

How well did the activity go? What stories work best for this activity? What was the effect of having an 'auditor' in each group? Do you know of any other interactive activities involving stories?

---

36 Testimony

Level	Advanced
Students	Adults
Purpose	Develop problem-solving ability; develop strategy of using information from other sources to help comprehension
Text type	Students' prepared texts; stories and accounts

In this activity ...

This is a 'jigsaw listening' activity. Students work in two different group formations, first (in 'expert groups') to gather testimony from different people and then (in 'jigsaw groups') to exchange information with other students.

Preparation

1. Prepare two different audio tapes, each of which gives one person's testimony about a problem (for example, two people who have information relevant to a civil or criminal case). A common example is a contract dispute between a landlord and a tenant: one testimony is the landlord's view, the other is the tenant's view. Prepare general comprehension questions to go with each tape extract.

> NOTE: *This type of jigsaw listening activity can be done with non-narrative topics as well. Possibilities are: differing views on the role of science and technology in society; differing accounts of a historical event; differing views on an environmental problem.*

2. Prepare a set of specific questions that you want the members of each 'testimony group' to ask each other, or a few general 'problem-solving' questions that the students can approach in various ways. (For example: who is at fault — the landlord or the tenant? Why?)

In class

1. Group the students into 'testimony groups'. They will need separate tape recorders

in separate parts of the room. Allot each group a fixed amount of time to listen to the testimony and answer comprehension questions.

2. Next, group the students into 'jigsaw groupings': pairs or groups of four, with each testimony represented in the jigsaw group by at least one person. Pose the questions that the jigsaw groups are to answer.

Variation 36.1: Fill the gap

One group listens to an excerpt from the beginning of a taped drama, the other group listens to an excerpt close to the ending. Students in the jigsaw groups attempt to work out a possible story line.

Variation 36.2: Assemble the script

Students work in jigsaw groups consisting of three members. One person in each group has access to a partial script from a video drama sequence; the second person has access to the audio soundtrack of the sequence; the third person has access to the video segment with no soundtrack (i.e. sound turned off). In their jigsaw groups, they 'assemble the script'. Finally, they verify with the video tape (with sound).

Follow-up options

1. Review the answers to the jigsaw group questions. Do all groups agree? What, if any, are the sources of disagreement? Can you iron these out by referring back to the original testimony?

2. Ask the students to recall, and to write out, any similar examples of 'disputes' which may lend themselves to a 'testimony' type of activity.

3. Prepare an extended 'simulation' activity in which the students learn background information about a problem (in their 'expert groups') and then role-play the solution (in their 'jigsaw groups').

Links

Consider trying activities 7, 14 and 18.1 as a follow-up to this activity.

Teacher's diary

Which aspects of the activity went well? Which did not go so well? What are some of the advantages and disadvantages of jigsaw learning activities?

---

37 Conversation tips

Level	Advanced
Students	Adults
Purpose	Develop strategy of listening for speaker's intention; develop ability to draw inferences from cues given
Text type	Audio tape; conversation

In this activity ...

Students identify different ways in which a listener can respond in a social conversation.

Preparation

1. Before class: write out several two-party conversations that might take place among friends. In each conversation, one person should be doing nearly all the talking. This person, the 'speaker', should be talking about a personal problem (e.g. a pushy boss, noisy neighbours, rising prices). The other person, the 'listener', should show one of the following 'attitudes' in each turn:
   (a) sympathetic (*e.g. Oh, that's too bad. Oh, no! Really?*)
   (b) interrogative (*e.g. Why did you do that? What did [he] say then?*)
   (c) suggestive (*e.g. Why don't you ...? If I were you, I would ...*)
   (d) evaluative (*e.g. I think that's unfair ... I think you were right in doing that ...*)

2. Tape these conversations. Ask a colleague to help you.

Sample tape segment

SPEAKER: *I'm having trouble with my neighbours ...*
LISTENER: *Oh, that's too bad.*
SPEAKER: *They're really not very friendly ... and they make a lot of noise! It sounds like a factory ... night and day ... constant noise.*
LISTENER: *Oh, I bet it's hard for you to study.*
SPEAKER: *It is. I have to go to the library to study ... even on Saturdays and Sundays.*
LISTENER: *That must be a lot of trouble for you.*

In class

1. How does the 'listener' respond to the speaker? Write out these four 'listener attitudes' on the blackboard:

   Type A: shows sympathy to the speaker.
   Type B: interrogates the speaker.
   Type C: gives suggestions to the speaker.
   Type D: evaluates what the speaker says.

   Elicit definitions of these phrases from the students, or provide brief definitions.

2. Introduce the situations and conversation topics. Then play the conversational extracts you have recorded. After the students have listened to each extract, ask them which of the attitudes the listener showed. Ask the students to recall expressions, intonation, or tone of voice that are associated with each type of listener attitude.

Variation 37.1: Listener diary

Ask the students to keep a listener diary for one week. Each day they should note down how they acted in different listening situations, both in their native language and in English. Can they identify different listening strategies they used or different listening 'attitudes' they had in these different situations? Can they identify any specific actions or words that were connected with these attitudes or strategies? Collect the diaries on a regular basis in order to get a clearer picture of how your students are developing their listening ability.

Follow-up options

1. Ask students to re-enact the conversations, selecting different listener attitudes from the ones provided in the tape sample.

2. Discuss with the students which listener attitudes they use most often in social conversations. Ask them which they prefer to use. Ask them if they find one or more of the attitudes culturally unacceptable in the situations portrayed on the tape.

3. Introduce the following topics in your class. They are also related to appropriate 'listener response':

   - Formal vs. informal expressions in different situations and with different people, showing respect for the person you are talking to.
   - Body contact, body distance, use of gestures during conversations, sitting and standing postures during conversations.

- Eye contact, direction of gaze during a conversation.
- Pace of speaking, volume of voice; tone of voice in conversations.

Present contrasting situations, using video tape if possible. Discuss which 'listener behaviour' seems to be more appropriate to the situation.

Links

Consider trying activities 8, 12.1, 21.1 and 22.1 as a follow-up to this activity.

Teacher's diary

How did the activity go? Did the activity lead to a discussion on the role of cultural expectations in social interaction? Did the activity suggest some aspects of conversational listening in which your students need practice?

INDEXES

A. Short summary of activities

(NB Activities are listed by title. Activity titles in **bold typeface** are main activities, indicated by chapter number. Activities in *italics* are variations to the main activities and are indicated by the letter V. followed by chapter number and the number of the variation.)

Add on (V.9.2). Students play a memory game, adding on to previous speaker's utterance.

Alternatives (12). Students identify differences in two spoken texts.

Angles (V.34.2). Students direct each other to position pictures on a grid.

Appropriateness (V.12.1). Students identify language of appropriateness in conversations.

Argument map (V.24.2). Students analyse the kind of argument that is used by a speaker.

Assemble the script (V.36.2). Students work in jigsaw groups to assemble the script of a video segment, then watch the video to verify their script.

Biography (V.31.1). Students are interviewed on topics related to their 'famous person' role.

Blindfolds (V.33.3). A student who is blindfolded listens to directions to find various objects in the room.

Blip! (V.6.1). Students ask clarification questions about missing information.

Boundaries (17). Students listen to utterances and mark the pause boundaries.

Cartoon sequences (V.34.1). Students receive different parts of a story and decide on the sequence.

Cartoon squares (V.33.2). Student instructs partner to assemble a cartoon sequence.

Classroom language (1). Students learn useful clarification language for classroom speaking and listening exercises.

Classroom management (V.1.1). Students learn to recognise useful language for classroom management routines.

Complete the story (V.35.1). Students provide a plausible ending to the story.

Contradiction game (V.20.2). Students listen for contradictions in a description or account.

Contrast (V.16.1). Students identify stress contrasts in utterances.

Conversation clues (28). Students listen to short conversations and make guesses about each conversation.

Conversation tips (37). Students identify different ways that a listener can respond in a social conversation.

Cues game (18). Students listen to cues and try to guess the target word.

Demonstrations (2). Students follow action sequences with props and visual aids.

Diagrams (V.33.1). Students explain to a partner how to construct a figure.

Discrimination (10). Students listen and point to object mentioned.

Documentary (V.23.1). Students predict, then verify, facts that appear in a video documentary.

Elicit the words (V.21.2). Students provide a song transcript from cues given.

Episode (29). Students listen to an episode from a TV drama and complete a comprehension check quiz.

Event squares (V.6.2). Students listen to short personal events and guess which classmate wrote each one.

Facts and figures (23). Students listen to factual descriptions and record the key information on grids.

Famous person (V.8.1). Students take the role of a famous person and give 'self-introductions'.

Fill the gap (V.36.1). Students receive information about different characters and then work in jigsaw groups to work out a possible story line.

Fixed forms (V.14.2). Students listen for specific grammatical forms.

Future plans (V.32.2). Students recall a sequence of activities.

Group survey (30). Students work in small groups to complete personal surveys.

Images (21). Students recall key words from a song that help create the song's images.

Impromptu speeches (V.32.1). Students work in groups to talk on topics with only brief preparation.

In order (26). Students listen to dialogues and put the lines in order.

Interruptions (V.5.2). Students interrupt the story-teller to ask for clarification.

Interview (8). Students are interviewed on prepared topics.

Jigsaw dictation (14). Students work in groups, taking dictation and comparing texts.

Just narration (V.4.1). Students listen to narration and ask questions.

Keep the pace (V.17.1). Students identify whether pause groups are read at fast, medium, or slow speed.

Leader says (V.2.1). Students play a game about following directions.

Listen for this! (V.21.1). Students identify phrases in a song.

Listener diary (V. 37.1). Students keep a 'listener diary', noting down how they reacted to different listening situations.

Listening skits (7). Students listen to directions in order to perform a skit.

Long or short? (V. 15.1). Students discriminate between unreduced and reduced forms.

Map route (33). Students work in pairs, with one directing the other how to arrive at a certain destination on the map.

Memory game (V.20.1). Students look at a picture, then they listen to a description and evaluate statements about the picture as correct or incorrect.

Monologues (V.26.1). Students listen to monologues and put the segments in order.

Music images (3). Students listen to music extracts and write down images.

News vocabulary (V.12.2). Students listen for specific vocabulary items in a broadcast.

Odd one out (V.10.2). Students listen and decide which item does not belong.

One, two, three (V.15.3). Students identify the order in which they heard the stressed words in a sentence.

One-sided conversations (11). Students work out missing lines in a conversation.

Opinion gap (V.25.2). Students identify and discuss arguments of speakers in a debate.

Pair dictation (V.14.1). Students dictate parts of a passage to each other.

Paraphrase (13). Students provide paraphrases of target lines in a dialogue.

Passages (V.9.3). Students listen to short passages on take-home tapes.

Personal stories (4). Students listen to narration and ask questions.

Picture differences (34). Students work in pairs to discover differences between a set of pictures.

Predict the next part (V.24.1). Students make predictions about what will happen next in a story.

Project journalist (V.30.1). Students conduct interviews outside class and bring the results to class for compilation.

Question pauses (V.5.1). Students ask questions to elicit a story.

Questions, please! (5). Students ask questions to elicit a story.

Recorded messages (22). Students listen to messages and note down key information.

Recounted stories (35). Students retell stories to other students; the 'listener' student is provided with a list of questioning prompts.

Reduced and expanded stories (V.12.3). Students identify which segments of a story are additions.

Replacements (V.12.4). Students identify changes in a story which alter the meaning.

Say it again (9). Students listen to and repeat selected phrases.

Scenes (V.7.1). Students change a video scene to a 'listening skit' format.

Second word (V.15.2). Students write down the second word in an utterance, which has reduced stress.

Self-access (V.29.1). Students participate in a self-access listening programme.

Self-introductions (31). Students give short self-introductions and make brief notes about each classmate.

Sequence (V.10.1). Students listen and put pictures or words in order.

Service encounters (V.22.1). Students fill out information grids as they listen to situational conversations.

Short forms (15). Students practise recognising weak (reduced stress) forms of words in connected speech.

Short speeches (32). Students listen to each other give short prepared speeches and complete evaluation sheets.

Similar tunes (V.3.1). Students compare two pieces of music.

Sound bingo (V.19.2). Students listen to target sounds or words and cover pictures on a grid with a marker.

Sound sequences (19). Students listen to a sequence of sounds and imagine a setting and characters.

Sound skit (V.19.1). Students prepare a skit using only sound effects and perform it for the class.

Sound track (V.19.3). Students listen to the sound track from a scene in a film and list the sights that will be in the picture.

Standard questions (V.27.2). Students write their own test questions.

Statement or question? (V.16.2). Students identify rising vs. falling intonation patterns in sentences.

Story boards (V.5.3). Students listen to the teacher narrate a story with visual scenes and manipulable characters.

Story maps (24). Students hear a narrative and construct a 'map' of the story.

Stress (16). Students listen to sentences and identify the stressed syllables and words.

Talk show (25). Students listen to a segment of a talk show and identify topics and main points.

Teams (V.18.1). Students work in teams to listen to cues and try to guess the target word.

Telephone game (V.9.1). Students pass a verbal message around their group and then compare it with the original message.

Test prep (V.13.1). Students choose correct paraphrases of lines in a dialogue.

Test questions (V.28.2). Students write down 'inference links' between lines in a dialogue.

Testimony (36). Students work in two different group formations to gather testimony from different people and then exchange information.

That's not right! (20). Students look at a picture as they listen to a description and evaluate statements as correct or incorrect.

Topic listening (27). Students listen to short lectures on a given topic.

Video documentary (V.4.2). Students listen to documentary and answer questions.

Which was it? (V.28.1). Students select the *exact* line that the speaker used.

Who's who? (6). Students follow directions in order to fill out forms.

Whose line? (V.25.1). Students categorise phrases in a dialogue by speaker.

Word chains (V.11.1). Students identify cohesion links in a conversation.

Write your questions (V.27.1). Students write down one question each about a lecture segment.

B. Type of student activity

(NB These headings indicate the main type of student activity that is promoted by the basic activity. In all activities — and especially in the variations and the follow-ups — the students will perform other actions as well.)

Answering questions

Conversation clues 111
Famous person 45
Interview 44
Self-access 115
Service encounters 95
Story boards 36
Test questions 112
Testimony 142
That's not right! 89
Topic listening 108

Asking questions (by the students)

Future plans 131
Group survey 124
Interruptions 36
Just narration 33
Personal stories 32
Project journalist 125
Question pauses 36
Questions, please! 35
Self-introductions 127
Short speeches 130
Standard questions 109
Video documentary 33
Write your questions 109

Clarifying

Classroom language 24
Map route 133
Diagrams 134
Cartoon squares 135
Picture differences 136
Cartoon sequences 137
Angles 137
Recounted stories 139

Completing gapped passages

Episode 114
Pair dictation 68
Jigsaw dictation 67

Completing grids

Facts and figures 97
Recorded messages 94
Service encounters 95
Documentary 98
Short speeches 130
Video documentary 33
Story maps 100
Argument map 101

Detecting differences

Alternatives 61
Contradiction game 90
Contrast 74
Keep the pace 77
One, two, three 71
Reduced and expanded stories 63
Replacements 63
Short forms 70
Stress 73

Dictation

Fixed forms 68
Jigsaw dictation 67
Pair dictation 68

Evaluating

Short speeches 130
Impromptu speeches 131
Self-access 115
Opinion gap 104

Filling in forms

Who's who? 38
Short speeches 130
Recorded messages 94

Following directions

Blindfolds 135
Classroom management 25
Demonstrations 26
Leader says 27

Listening skits 41
Who's who? 38

Games

Add on 53
Blindfolds 135
Cues game 84
Leader says 27
Odd one out 56
Sound bingo 87
Teams 84
Telephone game 53

Grammar practice

Alternatives 61
Elicit the words 93
Fixed forms 68
Jigsaw dictation 67
Listen for this! 92
One, two, three 71
Pair dictation 68
Paraphrase 64
Second word 71
Statement or question? 74
Stress 73
Test prep 65
Word chains 59

Identifying lines

Say it again 52
Listen for this! 92
Which was it? 112
Talk show 103
Whose line? 104

Identifying main ideas

Talk show 103
Topic listening 108

Identifying sounds and words

Contrast 74
Discrimination 55
'Long or short?' 71

Second word 71
Short forms 70
Sound bingo 87
Stress 73

Making inferences

Assemble the script 143
Cues game 84
Event squares 39
Fill the gap 143
Odd one out 56
One-sided conversations 58
Paraphrase 64
Sound sequences 86
Sound track 87

Memorising

In order 106
Passages 53

Noting impressions

Impromptu speeches 131
Music images 29
Short speeches 130

Note-taking

Project journalist 125
Topic listening 108

Ordering (putting items in order)

Cartoon squares 135

In order 106
Monologues 107
Sequence 56
Sound sequences 86

Paraphrasing

Paraphrase 64
Test prep 65
Which was it? 112

Predicting

Complete the story 140
One-sided conversations 58
Predict the next part 101

Repeating

Boundaries 76
Say it again 52

Recalling

Future plans 131
Memory game 90
Recounted stories 139

Role play

Listening skits 41
Sequence 56
Sound skit 87

Transcribing

Classroom language 24

Classroom management 25
Jigsaw dictation 67
Pair dictation 68
Scenes 42

Transferring information

Biography 128
Scenes 42

Visualising

Images 92
Memory game 90
Music images 29
Passages 53

Vocabulary building

Alternatives 61
Cues game 84
Discrimination 55
Elicit the words 93
News vocabulary 62
Odd one out 56
Replacements 63
Word chains 59

Written quizzes

Episode 114
Topic listening 108

C. Sources for the activities

(NB This list indicates the source or 'text type' used in the activity.)

Conversations

Appropriateness 62
Conversation clues 111
Conversation tips 144
In order 106
Paraphrase 64
Service encounters 95
Short forms 70
Whose line? 104
Word chains 59

Descriptions

Discrimination 55
Memory game 90
Sequence 56
That's not right! 89

Debate

Argument map 101
Opinion gap 104
Talk show 103
Testimony 142

Documentaries

Documentary 98
News vocabulary 62
Video documentary 33

Drama

Assemble the script 143
Listening skits 41
Say it again 52
Scenes 42
Self-access 115
Sound sequences 86
Sound skit 87

Games

Add on 53
Blindfolds 135
Contradiction game 90
Cues game 84
Leader says 27
Odd one out 56
Sound bingo 87
Teams 84
Telephone game 53

Instructions

Demonstrations 26
Leader says 27
Listening skits 41
Scenes 42
Who's who? 38

Interviews

Famous person 45
Interview 44
Project journalist 125
Talk show 103

Lectures

Demonstration 26
Topic listening 108

Messages

Facts and figures 97
Recorded messages 94

Music/songs

Elicit the words 93
Images 92
Listen for this! 92
Similar tunes 30

News broadcasts

News vocabulary 62
Replacements 63

Pictures

Angles 137
Cartoon sequences 137
Cartoon squares 135
Diagrams 134
Discrimination 55
Map route 133
Memory game 90
Sequence 56
Story boards 36

Poetry

Jigsaw dictation 67
Pair dictation 68
Passages 53

Prose passages

Alternatives 61
Argument map 101
Fixed forms 68
Jigsaw dictation 67
Pair dictation 68
Passages 53
Replacements 63

Speeches

Biography 128
Impromptu speeches 131
Self-introductions 127
Short speeches 130

Stories/narratives

Alternatives 61
Complete the story 140
Fill the gap 143
Future plans 131
Just narration 33
Monologues 107
Personal stories 32
Predict the next part 101
Questions, please! 35
Reduced and expanded stories 63
Story maps 100

Surveys

Group survey 124
Project journalist 125

Telephone conversations

One-sided conversations 58
Recorded messages 94

Tests

Conversation clues 111
Standard questions 109
Test prep 65
Test questions 112
Topic listening 108

D. Recommended activities by language proficiency level
(beginning, intermediate, advanced)

(NB Most activities can be adapted for students at different levels of proficiency. The list here indicates those activities which are most readily suited for students of the given proficiency levels. Activities in **bold typeface** are main activities.)

Beginning students

Add on 53
Blindfolds 135
Blip! 39

Classroom language 24

Classroom management 25
Contradiction game 90

Cues game 84

Demonstrations 26

Discrimination 55

Facts and figures 97

Fixed forms 68

Images 92

Interview 44

Leader says 27
Listen for this! 92
Listener diary 145

Listening skits 41

'Long or short?' 71
Odd one out 56
Pair dictation 68
Passages 53

Personal stories 32

Picture differences 136

Questions, please! 35

Recorded messages 94

Say it again 52

Self-introduction 127

Sequence 56

Short forms 70

Similar tunes 30
Sound bingo 87

Sound sequences 86

Statement or question? 74
Stress 73
Teams 84
Telephone game 53

That's not right! 89

Which was it? 112

Intermediate students

Alternatives 61

Angles 137
Biography 128
Boundaries 76
Cartoon sequence 137
Cartoon squares 135

Classroom language 24

Classroom management 25
Complete the story 140
Contradiction game 90
Contrast 74

Conversation clues 111

Demonstrations 26

Diagrams 134

Elicit the words 93
Event squares 39

Facts and figures 97

Famous person 45
Fill the gap 143
Fixed forms 68
Future plans 131

Group survey 124

Images 92

In order 106

Interview 44

Jigsaw dictation 67

Keep the pace 77
Listen for this! 92
Listener diary 145

Map route 133

Memory game 90
Monologues 107

Music images 29

One-sided conversations 58

Opinion gap 104
Pair dictation 68

Paraphrase 64

Passages 53

Personal stories 32

Picture differences 136

E. Recommended activities by student age (children 8–12; young adults 13–17; adults 18 and over)

(NB Nearly all activities can be adapted for students of different ages. The list here presents those activities which are most readily suited to students of the given age group. Activities in **bold typeface** are main activities.)

F. Medium used in the activity
(audio tape, video tape, or 'live interaction')

(NB Many of these can also be done with a live 'recital' by the teacher. Activities in **bold typeface** are main activities.)

Activities utilising audio tapes

Alternatives (12) 61

Appropriateness (V.12.1) 62
Argument map (V.24.2) 101

Conversation clues (28) 111

Discrimination (10) 55

Documentary (V.23.1) 98
Elicit the words (V.21.2) 93

Episode (29) 114

Facts and figures (23) 97

Images (21) 92

in order (26) 106

Listen for this! (V.21.1) 92
'Long or short?' (V.15.1) 71
Monologues (V.26.2) 107

Music images (3) 29

News vocabulary (V.12.2) 62

One-sided conversations (11) 58

Opinion gap (V.25.2) 104

Paraphrase (13) 64

Passages (V.9.3) 53
Predict the next part (V.24.1) 101

Recorded messages (22) 94

Replacements (V.12.4) 63

Say it again (9) 52

Self-access (V.29.1) 115

Sequence (V.10.1) 56
Service encounters (V.22.1) 95

Short forms (15) 70

Similar tunes (V.3.1) 30
Sound bingo (V.19.2) 87

Sound sequences (19) 86

Standard questions (V.27.2) 109

Story maps (24) 100

Talk show (25) 103

Test prep (V.13.1) 65
Test questions (V.28.2) 112

Testimony (36) 142

Topic listening (27) 10⁹

Which was it? (V.28.1) 112
Whose line? (V.25.1) 104
Word chains (V.11.1) 59
Write your questions (V.27.1) 109

Activities utilising video tapes

Assemble the script (V.36.2) 143
Documentary (V.23.1) 98

Episode (29) 114

In order (26) 106

Listen for this! (V.21.1) 92
News vocabulary (V.12.2) 62
Opinion gap (V.25.2) 104
Predict the next part (V.24.1) 101

Say it again (9) 52

Scenes (V.7.1) 42

Self-access (V.21.1) 115
Sequence (V.10.1) 56
Sound track (V.19.3) 87
Standard questions (V.27.2) 109

Story maps (24) 100

Talk show (25) 103

Topic listening (27) 108

Video documentary (V.4.2) 33
Whose line? (V.25.1) 104
Write your questions (V.27.1) 109

Activities for 'live' interaction (teacher–student or student–student)

Add on (V.9.2) 53

Alternatives (12) 61

Angles (V.34.2) 137
Biography (V.31.1) 128
Blindfolds (V.33.3) 135
Blip! (V.6.1) 39

Boundaries (17) 76

Cartoon squences (V.34.1) 137
Cartoon squares (V.33.2) 135

Classroom language (1) 24

Classroom management (V.1.1) 25
Complete the story (V.35.1) 140
Contradiction game (V.20.2) 90

Conversation tips (37) 144

Cues game (18) 84

Demonstrations (2) 26

161

92706

LINCOLN CHRISTIAN COLLEGE AND SEMINARY